Caprial's
BISTRO STYLE CUISINE

THIS BOOK BELONGS TO

....

Caprial's
BISTRO STYLE CUISINE

CAPRIAL PENCE

PHOTOGRAPHY BY
EDWARD GOWANS

TEN SPEED PRESS
BERKELEY, CALIFORNIA

1⊘

Ten Speed Press
Box 7123
Berkeley, California 94707
www.tenspeed.com

Distributed in Australia by Simon & Schuster Australia, in Canada by Ten Speed Press Canada, in New Zealand by Tandem Press, in South Africa by Real Books, in Southeast Asia by Berkeley Books, and in the United Kingdom and Europe by Airlift Books.

Cover and text design by Assumpta Curry, Tiburon, California.
Headnote and sidebar writing assistance by Gail Meredith, Portland, Oregon.
Food photography by Edward Gowans, Portland, Oregon.
Front cover photo and back flap photo by Jerome Hart, Portland, Oregon.
Food styling by Heather Bowen, Portland, Oregon.
Illustrations by Monica Dengo, San Francisco, California.

Special thanks to those who kindly loaned props:
Carl Greve, Portland, Oregon, for props used in the photos of Grilled Shrimp and Sausage with Apple-Brandy Glaze; Chile and Tomato Saifun Noodle Salad; Chilled Mango-Curry Soup; Pork Roast Stuffed with Pecan Stuffing; Lamb Shanks Braised with Roasted Shallots and Dried Cherries; Double-Crust Mushroom Pie; Seared Curried Eggplant; Polenta & Pesto Lasagne; John's Lemon Curd and Blueberry Cheesecake; Chocolate Truffle Tart; Mixed Berry Turnovers; Caramelized Banana Cream Pie.
Patrick Horsley, Portland, Oregon, for props used in the photos of Chile and Tomato Saifun Noodle Salad; Grilled Vegetable Shish Kabobs with Sherry Peppercorn Marinade; Seared Curried Eggplant.

Library of Congress Cataloging-in-Publication Data
Pence, Caprial
    [Bistro-Style cuisine]
    Caprial's bistro-style cuisine / Caprial Pence : photography by
Edward Gowans.
            p.   cm.
    Includes index.
    ISBN 0-89815-946-6
    1. Cookery.   I. Title.
    TX714.P4448   1997
    641.5—dc21   97-35444
                                                        CIP

Printed in the United States.
First printing, 1998

2 3 4 5 6 7 8 9 10 — 02 01 00 99

Contents

To Mom and Dad,
who have always loved, encouraged,
and taught me.

Acknowledgments

Thanks to the whole Bistro staff for all the hard work, and for answering the endless phone calls and questions. To my husband, John, and our children, Alex and Savannah, thanks for letting me do what I love. To all the staff and crew who worked on the television series, I couldn't have done it without you. To Lorena, my editor, thanks for putting up with me and helping me create a great book.

Introduction

Some years back, when my husband John and I were working our hearts out at high-profile jobs in Seattle kitchens, we decided we wanted to slow down and enjoy life more. So, with plans to open a cozy neighborhood restaurant, we packed up and moved to Portland, where I grew up and my family was still rooted. Our concept was simple: We would work with local farmers and other small suppliers to find the best foods we could afford to serve. We'd make beautiful food with bright, bold flavors, drawing inspiration from the world's cuisines.

In 1992, our plan materialized when we opened the Westmoreland Bistro, so-named for the neighborhood in which it's nestled. It was an unassuming, 26-seat restaurant with the menu scribbled on a chalkboard. After three years (and some wonderful reviews!), John talked me into changing the name to Caprial's Bistro, so people could find us more easily. Now, four cookbooks, four television cooking series, and countless cooking classes and catering jobs later, it seems we haven't really slowed down at all. But our life is richer and more fun than we'd ever imagined it could be back when we were young chefs in Seattle.

I base the recipes in my books and on my cooking shows on the actual dishes we serve at Caprial's, which John and I run together with the help and creativity of our chef, Mark Dowers. However, as a mother of two who, like most everyone else, has to squeeze in time to cook at home, I understand that no one has the luxury to go through all the steps we do when preparing a dish at the Bistro. With that in mind, I've simplified a selection of our most popular recipes for this book. It has always been one of my main goals to help home cooks build a repertoire of quick-to-make, sophisticated, down-to-earth dishes that they can cook for friends and family—and still have the time and energy to enjoy themselves when the cooking is done.

My cooking style, and the recipes in this book, grew out of the French tradition of the bistro—small neighborhood restaurants that serve simple, delicious food that comes together in a flash. (The word *bistro* reportedly entered the French lexicon in 1815, when Russian soldiers, who were loitering about Parisian cafes following the Battle of Waterloo, ordered waiters to bring their food "bystro! bystro!" or "quickly! quickly!")

But the traditional bistro is more than just a restaurant. It's also a comfortable place where people can be alone with their thoughts or pull up a chair to a boisterous table and laugh out loud as they enjoy their meal. Thankfully, bistro-style restaurants such as Caprial's are now found in neighborhoods all over the world.

By writing this book and doing the cooking shows, I hope to bring the spirit of Caprial's Bistro to your neighborhood and kitchen, showing how food and wine can draw us to the table and enrich our lives in simple, meaningful ways. To those who are concerned about the perceived physical tolls of enjoying wonderful food, I say that well-prepared, wholesome foods eaten in moderation are heathy for the body and soul. In defense of good food, I must point out that although we're consuming all these fat-free, sugar-free, additive-laden foods, we're not getting any thinner or healthier. At the bistro and in our home, I combat this by cooking locally grown, unprocessed seasonal foods and savoring their natural goodness. I hope the recipes in this book will show you how to apply the same concepts to your cooking and expand your taste for truly great food. Here's to more great cooking!

Glossary of Terms & Ingredients

Blanch: To partially cook briefly in boiling water.

Bok choy *(and baby bok choy)*: Also called Chinese white cabbage, bok choy is a dark green cabbage that somewhat resembles Swiss chard; baby bok choy is a smaller, more tender variety.

Butterfly: To cut a piece of meat nearly all the way through and open it out to make it twice as long but half as thick as it originally was. The meat should then be pounded flat with a meat mallet.

Caramelize: To cook sugar or an ingredient with a naturally high sugar content (such as some vegetables and meats) over high heat to brown the natural sugars and develop a deeper flavor.

Celeriac: Also know as celery root, this root vegetable has a celery-like flavor.

Chile paste: A Chinese condiment made from fermented fava beans, red chiles, and, sometimes, garlic.

Chile sauce: A sweet-hot Thai sauce made of chiles, sugar, and vinegar. Available in specialty markets.

Chorizo sausage: A spicy Mexican sausage made with pork and beef and seasoned with chile. Available in specialty markets and many supermarkets.

Crème fraîche: Cream combined with sour cream (or buttermilk) that is left out at room temperature for 8 to 24 hours, then refrigerated until thick.

Crystallized ginger: Also known as candied ginger. Available in most grocery stores and in Asian markets.

Curry paste: A mixture of ghee (clarified butter), vinegar, and curry powder used to flavor Indian and Asian dishes. Sold in gourmet and specialty markets.

Durkee's cayenne sauce: A vinegar-based, tangy, spicy sauce. I like to add it to soups, sauces, marinades, and salsas.

Emulsify: To completely blend together an oil or fat with an acid such as vinegar or lemon juice.

Fish sauce: A thin sauce made from fermented salted sardines or other fish. For more information, see page 12.

Fermented black beans: Small black soybeans preserved with salt. They have a distinct pungency and strong salty taste. Widely used in Chinese cooking. I rinse them before using.

Hot-smoked salmon: Salmon that is cooked as well as smoked (as opposed to cold-smoked salmon—like lox—which is smoked but not cooked).

Instant sour paste: A potent Asian flavoring paste that adds complexity to many dishes. I prefer the Tom Yum brand, which I use like salt and pepper. It keeps indefinitely in the refrigerator.

Julienne: Cut into matchsticks about $^{1}/8$ inch (3 mm) across by 2 inches (5 cm) long.

Kalamata olives: Smooth-skinned, dark purple, brine-cured Greek olives with an intense taste.

Kosher salt: Pure salt with an even, coarse texture; more soluble than table salt. Available in specialty markets and most supermarkets.

Lemongrass: A standard herb in Vietnamese and Thai cooking. Use fresh lemongrass for cooking; dried lemongrass is mainly used for tea. Available in Asian markets and some supermarkets.

Masa harina: Flour made from masa, which is corn that is fire dried and ground. Used to make dough for tamales.

Mascarpone: Double or triple cream from Italy. Slightly sweet and very rich.

Mesclun: Mixed wild salad greens.

Nonreactive bowl/pan/container: Made of glass, ceramic, or stainless steel. Metal components in aluminum and cast-iron can react with the acids in ingredients resulting in an off flavor.

Pancetta: Unsmoked, peppered Italian bacon. Available in gourmet markets.

Parchment paper: Oil- and moisture-resistant paper used to line baking sheets and pans to prevent baked items from sticking.

Pepper bacon: Bacon with a peppery crust.

Pickled ginger: Common Japanese condiment. Very thinly sliced ginger pickled in rice vinegar, salt, and spices. Commercial varieties are artificially colored.

Poblano chiles: Fresh, green form of the dried ancho chile. Spiciness ranges from medium to hot. Usually roasted before combining with other ingredients. Peak season is summer to early fall.

Prosciutto: Dry-cured, spiced Italian ham. Available in gourmet markets.

Reduce: To thicken and intensify the flavor of a sauce by boiling it down through evaporation.

Sabayon: Also known as zabaglione. A whipped custard of egg yolks, sugar, and sweet wine (or other alcohol).

Saifun noodles: Also known as glass noodles and bean thread noodles. Thin, transparent noodle made from mung beans.

Sectioning citrus: To remove the sections of oranges, tangerines, and mandarins from their membranelike coverings. For instructions, see page 192.

Shock: To submerge briefly in ice-cold water to stop the cooking process.

Tahini: Paste made from toasted sesame seeds; used in Middle Eastern cooking.

Tamarind paste: Sweet-sour paste made from the fruit of the pods of the tamarind tree.

Tapenade: A thick paste made from capers, anchovies, black olives, olive oil, and lemon juice.

Thai basil: Basil variety with green and maroon leaves and slightly spicy flavor.

Wasabi: Japanese green mustard, with similar flavor and usages as horseradish. Wasabi is very hot and pungent, and should be used sparingly. Available in powder and paste form in Asian and some supermarkets.

Wild mushrooms: All edible, nonpoisonous mushrooms that are indigenous to certain areas throughout the Pacific Northwest, among other regions. Some of the most common are chanterelles, enoki, morels, and shiitakes, which are all known for their particularly earthy qualities.

Appetizers

Beggar's Purses with Spicy Ratatouille & Garlic Crème Fraîche

EGGPLANT

I use a lot of eggplant in my cooking, and I particularly like the purple globe eggplants. Eggplant is a wonderful flavor carrier; it absorbs any flavor it is marinated or cooked in. For a marinade, I whisk together olive oil, garlic, and vinegar (balsamic is my favorite, but I sometimes use sherry vinegar).

The only time I salt eggplant (to draw out moisture and bitterness) is if I want to sear it to make it crisper for battering and frying. I salt eggplant slices well, then let them rest in a sieve for about 30 minutes while the liquid drips out.

I think it's unfortunate that crepes have gone out of vogue, so I created this recipe in an an effort to revive them. Be careful not to overcook the ratatouille or it will become mushy. If vine-ripened tomatoes are available, use them; if they're not, leave them out of the dish. For a vegetarian entrée, serve two purses per person along with a crisp green salad and crusty French bread. Keep in mind that the crème fraîche is quick to make, but needs to be prepared a day ahead.

GARLIC CRÈME FRAÎCHE

1 cup heavy whipping cream
1 tablespoon sour cream
2 cloves garlic, minced
2 teaspoons chopped fresh parsley
Salt
Freshly ground black pepper

CREPES

1 cup all-purpose flour
2/3 cup milk
2 eggs
2 cloves garlic
2 teaspoons butter, melted
Pinch of salt
1 tablespoon olive oil

RATATOUILLE

2 teaspoons olive oil
3 cloves garlic, chopped
1/2 red onion, diced
1 small eggplant, diced
1/2 cup sliced button mushrooms
1 small yellow squash, diced
1 small zucchini, diced
2 tomatoes, halved, seeded, and diced
1 roasted red bell pepper, peeled, seeded, and diced (page 190)
2 roasted poblano chiles, peeled, seeded, and diced (page 190)
2 teaspoons tomato paste
2 teaspoons chopped fresh basil
1 teaspoon chopped cilantro
Salt
Freshly ground black pepper

6 chives

To prepare the Garlic Crème Fraîche, combine the cream and sour cream in a small bowl and whisk together. Cover and let stand overnight at room temperature.

To prepare the crepes, place the flour, milk, and eggs in a blender and purée until smooth. Add the garlic, melted butter, and salt and purée again. Heat a few drops of the olive oil in an 8-inch nonstick sauté pan over high heat. Add about 2 tablespoons of crepe batter, or just enough to coat the bottom of the pan. Swirl the pan to evenly coat the bottom with the crepe batter. Cook until the crepe is golden brown, 2 to 3 minutes. Turn the crepe with a spatula and cook for about 30 seconds. Remove the crepe from the pan and set aside on a plate. Re-oil the pan and repeat with the remaining batter.

To prepare the ratatouille, heat the olive oil in a large sauté pan over high heat until very hot. Add the garlic and onion and sauté until fragrant, about 2 minutes. Add the eggplant and cook for about 3 minutes to sear, then turn and cook for another 3 minutes. Add the mushrooms, squash, zucchini, and tomatoes, and sauté for about 2 minutes. Add the bell peppers, poblanos, and tomato paste and stir to mix well. Add the basil and cilantro and cook for 3 to 4 minutes. Season to taste with the salt and pepper. Keep warm until ready to serve.

To finish the Garlic Crème Fraîche, add the garlic, parsley, salt, and pepper and mix well. Place in the refrigerator to chill completely before using, 1 to 2 hours.

When the crème fraîche is chilled, prepare the purses. Lay the crepes on a work surface. Divide the ratatouille evenly among them, placing it in the center of each one. Soak the chives in a bowl of very hot water for about 1 minute. Using your fingers, lift the sides of the crepes and gently tie them with a chive just above the filled bundle. Place 1 purse on each plate. Drizzle with the crème fraîche and serve warm or at room temperature.

When shopping for eggplant, choose ones that feel heavier than they look and pass up the female eggplants for the males; the females have too many seeds. To find the males, look at the tip of the eggplant: if there is an indentation, it is a female; a smooth roundness means it is a male. The slender Japanese eggplants have more tender skins and may be a bit more bitter than the large bulbous variety typically sold in markets. I like to split Japanese eggplants in half lengthwise, marinate the halves, and then grill them.

Apple Brandy–Glazed Shrimp & Sausage

SERVES 6

We grill almost nightly in summer, so we're always looking for new ideas. For this one, we wanted a real Northwest flavor, so we created a glaze based on an apple brandy made from our world-famous apples. I love this glaze—it's sweet and spicy and good with almost anything, from shrimp to pork tenderloin.

3 chorizo sausages or other spicy sausage

APPLE-BRANDY GLAZE
1 teaspoon olive oil
2 cloves garlic, chopped
1 teaspoon peeled, chopped fresh ginger
1/2 cup apple brandy
1/2 cup apple cider
2 tablespoons honey
1 jalapeño pepper, chopped
1/4 cup vegetable oil
1 teaspoon chopped fresh thyme
1 teaspoon cracked black pepper

12 medium shrimp, peeled, with tails

Preheat a grill. Set 6 wooden skewers to soak in water. Bring a stockpot of water to a boil. Add the sausage and blanch for 2 to 3 minutes, then transfer to a colander to cool.

To prepare the glaze, heat the olive oil in a sauté pan over high heat until hot. Add the garlic and ginger and sauté until fragrant, about 1 minute. Remove the pan from the heat, add the brandy, and return the pan to the burner. Cook until the brandy is reduced by about half, then add the apple cider and reduce again by half. Add the honey and jalapeño and cook for about 2 minutes. Remove from the heat, stir in the oil, thyme, and black pepper, then set aside to cool.

Cut the sausages on the diagonal into 4 pieces. Place 1 shrimp and 1 slice of sausage on a skewer, then repeat adding another shrimp and another piece of sausage. Repeat with the remaining skewers, shrimp, and sausage.

Place the skewers on the prepared grill and generously brush the top and sides with the glaze. After about 2 minutes, turn the skewers and brush them again with the glaze. Cook for another 2 minutes, until shrimp is just cooked through. Brush lightly with the glaze on all sides and serve.

Pissaladière

This is an updated version of a rustic French-style pizza. With fresh herbs, it becomes a satisfying, casual meal.

DOUGH

1 1/4 cups warm water

1 tablespoon active dry yeast

1/4 teaspoon sugar

1 tablespoon olive oil

2 teaspoons chopped fresh rosemary

1 teaspoon chopped fresh thyme

3 cloves garlic, chopped

3 cups all-purpose flour

1 teaspoon salt

TOPPING

10 whole shallots, halved lengthwise

10 cloves garlic

1/4 cup olive oil

2 oil or salt-packed anchovies, drained

2 tablespoons chopped fresh basil

1/4 cup balsamic vinegar

1 cup pitted, chopped kalamata olives

3 ounces Gorgonzola, crumbled

To prepare the dough, place 1/4 cup of the water, the yeast, and sugar in a bowl and mix well. Let the mixture proof until bubbling and foamy, about 5 minutes.

In the bowl of a heavy-duty mixer fitted with the paddle attachment, combine the remaining 1 cup of water, the oil, rosemary, thyme, and garlic and mix well. While mixing on slow speed, add the flour 1 cup at a time, waiting until each cup is incorporated before adding the next. When all of the flour is incorporated, add the salt and mix on slow speed for 4 to 5 minutes, or until a smooth, elastic dough forms. Transfer the dough to a well-floured work surface and knead to form a smooth ball. Place the dough in a well-greased bowl, cover with a kitchen towel, and let rise for about 1 1/2 hours, or until doubled in size.

Meanwhile, preheat the oven to 300°. Combine the shallots, garlic, and olive oil in an ovenproof sauté pan and roast for 1 hour, or until soft. Remove the shallots from the oven and let them cool. Transfer the shallots to the bowl of a food processor. Add the anchovies, basil, and vinegar, and purée. Set aside.

Preheat the oven to 425°. Lightly oil a 14-inch pizza pan. With lightly oiled hands, remove the dough from the bowl and stretch it out to 14 inches in circumference, to fit the pan. Using a spatula, spread the shallot mixture over the dough and sprinkle the olives over the top. Bake the pissaladière in the oven until the crust is golden brown, about 25 minutes. Sprinkle the Gorgonzola and remaining basil over the pissaladière, cut into 12 wedges, and serve.

Eggplant Caviar

SERVES 4

This roasted eggplant spread is great on grilled vegetable sandwiches; as a dip for raw vegetables, crackers, and triangles of pita bread or other flatbread; or as a spread for roasted pork butt or leg of lamb. My version is spicier and more flavorful than the traditional one.

> 1 large eggplant, halved lengthwise
> 1 tablespoon olive oil
> Salt
> Freshly ground black pepper
> 1 teaspoon freshly squeezed lemon juice
> 1/2 cup pine nuts, toasted (page 191)
> 1 tablespoon chopped fresh basil
> 1/4 cup chopped fresh tomatoes
> 1/2 teaspoon ground cayenne pepper
> 1/2 cup extra virgin olive oil

Preheat the oven to 425°. Using a sharp knife, score the flesh of the eggplant in a grid pattern, being careful not to cut through the skin. Drizzle the eggplant flesh with the olive oil and season with salt and pepper. Set the eggplant flesh down on a lightly oiled baking sheet and roast in the oven until tender, about 45 minutes. Remove from the oven and let cool.

Using a large spoon, scoop the eggplant flesh out of the skin and place it in the bowl of a food processor fitted with the metal blade. Add the lemon juice, pine nuts, basil, tomatoes, and cayenne pepper and process until smooth. With the machine running, slowly drizzle the extra virgin olive oil through the feeder tube and process until the mixture is thick. Season with salt and pepper. Serve at room temperature.

Wild Mushroom Strudel

SERVES 4

This recipe calls for chanterelles, but you can use any kind of wild mushrooms. Or, substitute white mushrooms and a few reconstituted dried wild mushrooms.

FILLING

1 tablespoon olive oil

1 small yellow onion, chopped

2 shallots, chopped

3 cloves garlic, chopped

1 cup red wine

4 cups sliced wild mushrooms

1/2 cup freshly grated Parmesan cheese

1/3 cup soft, mild goat cheese or ricotta cheese

1/4 cup toasted unseasoned bread crumbs

2 teaspoons chopped fresh basil

1 teaspoon chopped fresh rosemary

1/2 teaspoon cracked black pepper

Salt

4 sheets phyllo dough

4 tablespoons unsalted butter, melted

Roasted Red Bell Pepper & Basil Sauce (page 14)

Preheat the oven to 350°. Line a baking sheet with parchment paper.

To make the filling, heat the olive oil in a large sauté pan over high heat until very hot. Add the onion, shallots, and garlic and sauté until fragrant, about 1 minute. Add the red wine and reduce by half about 4 minutes. Add the mushrooms and cook until just tender and most of the liquid is reduced, 4 to 5 minutes. Remove the pan from the heat and allow the filling to cool slightly. Transfer the filling to a large bowl and allow it to cool completely. Fold in the Parmesan and goat cheeses. Add the bread crumbs, basil, rosemary, and black pepper. Mix well, season to taste with salt, and then set aside.

Place 2 sheets of the phyllo dough on a clean, dry work surface and generously brush the top sheet with melted butter. Place 2 more phyllo sheets on top and again brush the top sheet with butter. Spoon the filling into the center of the dough, spreading it to form a rectangle while leaving a 2-inch border. Fold one of the short ends of the dough about 1 inch over the filling. Fold one of the long ends over about 1 inch of the filling and gently roll into a log. Place the strudel, seam-side down, on the prepared baking sheet and cut 1/4-inch-deep vents along the top. Bake in the oven for 25 to 30 minutes, or until golden brown.

Remove the strudel from the oven and cool on the pan. Using a serrated knife, slice the strudel into 8 pieces. Serve warm with the sauce on the side.

Bruschetta with Gorgonzola Spread and a Trio of Tapenades

SERVES 6

OLIVES

I love olives. However, I don't particularly like salt-cured olives; their taste is too strong. For cooking, my olive of choice is the kalamata. Kalamatas are smooth, dark purple, brine-cured Greek olives with a tangy, rich, salty taste. My favorite green olive is the French picholine, which is mild and has just a hint of tang. They are especially tasty in green salads or as a simple appetizer along with cheese, crackers, and raw vegetables. Both olives are available in most supermarkets.

This is a very popular appetizer at the restaurant. We grill the olive oil–brushed French bread, spread on the garlic, add a layer of the creamy cheese spread, and top each piece with one of the three tapenades. Stacked on a serving platter, the tricolor bruschetta are as eye-catching as they are tasty. They're also an ideal way to use up day-old bread.

GORGONZOLA SPREAD

1/2 cup Gorgonzola
1/4 cup cream cheese
1/4 cup half-and-half

BLACK OLIVE TAPENADE

1/2 cup pitted cured black olives
2 cloves garlic
1/2 teaspoon capers
1 oil-packed anchovy fillet, drained
1 teaspoon freshly squeezed lemon juice
2 tablespoons olive oil

GREEN OLIVE TAPENADE

1/2 cup pitted cured green olives
2 cloves garlic
1/2 teaspoon capers
1 oil- or salt-packed anchovy fillet
1 teaspoon freshly squeezed lemon juice
2 tablespoons olive oil

SUNDRIED TOMATO TAPENADE

2/3 cup chopped dry-packed sun dried tomatoes
2 cloves garlic
2 teaspoons tomato purée
1 teaspoon capers
2 teaspoons chopped fresh basil
1/4 cup olive oil
Salt
Freshly ground black pepper

12 large slices good-quality French bread
1 tablespoon olive oil
3 cloves garlic, minced

To prepare the Gorgonzola Spread, place the Gorgonzola and cream cheese in the bowl of a food processor fitted with the metal blade and blend until creamy. Add the half-and-half and blend just until smooth. Set aside.

To prepare the Black Olive Tapenade, put the olives, garlic, capers, anchovy, and lemon juice in the bowl of the food processor and process until smooth. With the machine running, slowly add the olive oil through the feeder tube and process until smooth. Scrape down the sides of the bowl, place the mixture in a separate bowl, and set aside.

To prepare the Green Olive Tapenade, follow the instructions for the Black Olive Tapenade.

To prepare the Sundried Tomato Tapenade, place the tomatoes, garlic, tomato purée, capers, and basil in the bowl of the food processor and process until smooth. With the machine running, slowly add the olive oil through the feeder tube and process until smooth. Scrape down the sides of the bowl, season to taste with the salt and black pepper, and set aside.

To prepare the bruschetta, drizzle the bread slices with the olive oil and spread with a thin layer of the minced garlic. On a hot, well-oiled grill or under a broiler, grill the bread until crispy and brown. Remove the bread from the grill or broiler. Spread some of the Gorgonzola Spread on each slice. Spread the black olive tapenade on 4 slices. On another 4 slices, spread the green olive tapenade. Spread the remaining slices with the sundried tomato tapenade. Cut each slice into 3 triangles, place on a platter, and serve immediately.

Chicken & Shrimp Dumplings with Soy Dipping Sauce

SERVES 6

I love Asian dumplings of all kinds. These are so delicious and such fun to eat that John and I ate the whole batch when we tested the recipe!

SOY DIPPING SAUCE

1/2 cup soy sauce

2 tablespoons rice vinegar

2 tablespoons sweet hot chile sauce

2 slices peeled fresh ginger

24 wonton wrappers

1 tablespoon vegetable oil

1/2 cup chicken stock

1/4 cup water

FILLING

4 ounces ground chicken

6 medium shrimp, peeled and minced

2 cloves garlic, chopped

2 teaspoons peeled, chopped fresh ginger

1 green onion, chopped

2 teaspoons chopped fresh basil

1 tablespoon sweet hot chile sauce

Soy sauce

To prepare the sauce, put all of the ingredients in a small saucepan and bring to a boil. Remove the pan from the heat and set aside.

To prepare the filling, combine the chicken and shrimp in a small bowl and mix well. Add the ginger, garlic, green onion, basil, and chile sauce, mix well, and season to taste with soy sauce.

Lay a wonton wrapper on a work surface. Place 1 heaping teaspoon of the filling in the center of the wrapper. Bring the sides of the wrapper up around the filling to a point at the top, pleating the sides. Repeat with the remaining wrappers and filling.

In a large, nonstick sauté pan, add the oil and heat over high heat until very hot. Gently place the dumplings in the pan and cook until browned, about 2 minutes. Add the chicken stock and water and steam for about 2 minutes, or until tender. Remove the dumplings from the pan and serve hot with the dipping sauce.

Spicy Corn Muffins with Shrimp Salsa

SERVES 6

As a variation, I often bake this batter in old-fashioned corn-stick pans.

1/2 teaspoon salt

1 cup cornmeal

1 cup all-purpose flour

1 tablespoon sugar

1 tablespoon chopped fresh basil

1 teaspoon chopped cilantro

3 chopped jalapeño peppers

1 teaspoon baking powder

1 teaspoon chile powder

1 teaspoon ground cumin

3 cloves garlic, chopped

1 cup milk

1/4 cup vegetable oil

2 eggs

SHRIMP SALSA

1 tablespoon olive oil

8 large shrimp, peeled and diced

1/2 small onion, diced

3 cloves garlic, chopped

3 large tomatoes, seeded and diced

2 roasted red bell peppers, peeled, stemmed, seeded, & diced (page 190)

2 roasted poblano chiles, peeled, stemmed, & seeded (page 190)

Zest and juice of 1 lime

2 tablespoons rice vinegar

1/3 cup vegetable oil

2 teaspoons ground cumin

1 teaspoon chile powder

1 teaspoon ground coriander

1 teaspoon chopped cilantro

Salt

Freshly ground black pepper

1/2 cup sour cream

1 tablespoon chopped flat-leaf parsley

Preheat the oven to 350°. Grease 6 muffin cups or line with paper liners.

Combine the salt, cornmeal, flour, sugar, basil, cilantro, jalapeños, baking powder, chile powder, cumin, and garlic in a large bowl and mix well. In a separate bowl, whisk together the milk, vegetable oil, and eggs. Add the wet mixture to the dry mixture and stir just to combine. Pour the batter into the muffin cups and bake until golden brown, 15 to 20 minutes. Let cool in the pan, then remove.

To prepare the salsa, heat the olive oil in a sauté pan over high heat until very hot. Add the shrimp and cook for 2 to 3 minutes, or just until they turn pink. Remove the shrimp from the pan and let cool. When cool, put the shrimp in a large bowl. Add the onion, garlic, tomatoes, bell peppers, and poblanos, and toss well. In a small bowl, combine the lime zest, lime juice, rice vinegar, vegetable oil, cumin, chile powder, coriander, and cilantro and mix well. Add the dressing to the shrimp mixture and toss well. Season to taste with the salt and pepper.

To serve, split open the muffins and place on plates. Top the muffins with some of the salsa, a dollop of sour cream, and a sprinkling of the parsley. Serve warm.

Bistro Mussels with Vietnamese Sauce

SERVES 4

FISH SAUCE

Fish sauce is an essential ingredient in Thai cooking that adds depth, body, and substance, to dishes. Pungent and salty, it ranges in color from dark mustard to deep brown and in flavor from spicy to sweet. Like soy sauce it is used as a condiment and for flavoring.

Fish sauce is most commonly made from salted, fermented sardines. The Romans used a flavoring called "garum" that was much like soy sauce and perhaps a precursor to today's fish sauce. Fish sauce is available in Asian markets. The sauce stores well in the refrigerator for up to one year.

We love mussels and almost always have a mussel dish at the Bistro. The sauce is based on a Vietnamese recipe, but we've added oomph to make it extra tangy and spicy. We also like to use this sauce with clams and for poaching salmon and cod.

VIETNAMESE SAUCE
1 tablespoon chopped garlic
2 tablespoons peeled, julienned fresh ginger
3 cups fish stock (page 187)
1 tablespoon tamarind paste, seeds removed
1 tablespoon instant sour paste (optional)
1/4 cup finely ground, peeled fresh lemongrass
Zest of 1 lime
3 tablespoons freshly squeezed lime juice
4 dashes fish sauce
1 heaping teaspoon chile paste
1/4 cup cornstarch

3 pounds mussels, scrubbed and debearded

To prepare the sauce, place the garlic, ginger, and fish stock in a large saucepan and bring to a boil over high heat. Add the tamarind paste, sour paste, ground lemongrass, zest, and lime juice. Reduce the heat and simmer, uncovered, for about 10 minutes to reduce slightly. Add the fish sauce and chile paste and stir well. Put the cornstarch in a small bowl and stir in enough cold water to soften it. Return the sauce to a boil over high heat and whisk the cornstarch into the boiling sauce. Taste, adjust seasonings, and set aside.

To prepare the mussels, place them in a large stockpot. Add the sauce and cook over high heat for about 10 minutes, or until the mussels open. Place the mussels in a large bowl and pour the sauce over the top. Serve hot.

Crab Cocktail with Chipotle Sauce

SERVES 4

This is a beautiful dish for summer gatherings on the deck or patio. The crunch of the thinly sliced cucumber contrasts well with the smooth, soft crab, and the spicy chipotle sauce balances the crab's sweet, mild flavor. Your guests will love the cocktail's formal flair.

CHIPOTLE SAUCE
2 cloves garlic, chopped
1 shallot, chopped
3/4 cup chile sauce
1 teaspoon ground cumin
1/2 teaspoon ground coriander
1/2 teaspoon chile powder
1 small chipotle chile
1 teaspoon chopped fresh basil
Salt
Cracked black pepper

1 small cucumber, thinly sliced
2 cups Dungeness crabmeat
   or local crab
Minced zest and juice of 1 lemon
2 green onions, minced

To prepare the sauce, place the garlic, shallot, and chile sauce in the bowl of a food processor fitted with the metal blade and purée well. Add the cumin, coriander, chile powder, chile, and basil and purée well. Season to taste with salt and black pepper, mix well, and set aside.

To prepare the cocktail, line 4 martini glasses with the thinly sliced cucumber. Put the crab, zest, juice, and green onions in a medium bowl and toss well. Divide the crab mixture among the 4 glasses and top with a dollop of cocktail sauce. Serve cold.

Smoked Chicken Tamales with Spicy Roasted Red Bell Pepper–Basil Sauce

SERVES 6

CILANTRO

Cilantro is the Spanish name for Chinese parsley and fresh coriander. Commonly used in Asian, Latin American, and Caribbean cooking, the delicate-looking cilantro leaves have a distinctive, somewhat spicy flavor that some liken to soap. A little goes a long way, and it's easy to overdo it and spoil a dish—for that reason I call it "devil herb." I use it sparingly as a garnish on dishes that need a little bite. Cilantro tastes better fresh than cooked; when cooked, the flavor fades and the herb looks tired. When shopping for

This spicy, contemporary tamale evolved from an experience I had in an over-priced, trendy restaurant: I was served a really bad tamale. Tamales deserve better! I have tried many different kinds of tamale fillings, but I've returned to a traditional approach with just a few variations, such as using basil instead of cilantro and substituting roasted red bell peppers for tomatoes. If you prefer, serve the tamales with salsa instead of the red bell pepper sauce. If you want to make this hot appetizer ahead, just wrap and refrigerate the tamales and steam them right before serving. Look for the corn husks in the Mexican foods section of your supermarket or in Latin American markets.

ROASTED RED BELL PEPPER & BASIL SAUCE

4 red bell roasted, peppers, peeled, seeded, and diced (page 190)
2 cloves garlic, chopped
1 tablespoon chopped fresh basil
1 chipotle chile, stemmed
2 tablespoons Durkee's cayenne sauce
1/2 teaspoon ground cumin
Salt

TAMALE DOUGH

1 1/2 cups masa harina
1/2 teaspoon sugar
1/2 teaspoon salt
1 teaspoon melted butter
1 clove garlic, chopped
3/4 cup water

FILLING

1 teaspoon vegetable oil
1/2 pound boneless smoked chicken, diced
2 cloves garlic, chopped
4 New Mexican chiles, roasted, peeled, stemmed, seeded, and coarsely chopped (page 190)
1/4 cup grated Monterey jack cheese
1/4 cup grated Cheddar cheese
1 teaspoon ground cumin
1/2 teaspoon ground coriander
1/2 teaspoon chile powder
Salt and pepper

8 large corn husks

To prepare the sauce, combine all of the ingredients in a blender or in the bowl of a food processor fitted with the metal blade and purée until smooth. Set aside until ready to serve, or store in an airtight container in the refrigerator for up to 1 week.

To prepare the dough, in a mixing bowl combine the masa, sugar, salt, butter, garlic, and water and stir until a soft dough forms. Cover with plastic wrap and set aside.

To prepare the filling, place the oil in a large sauté pan over high heat and heat until smoking hot. Add the chicken and cook until almost cooked through, about 4 minutes. Add the garlic and chiles and toss to combine well. Remove the pan from the heat and let cool. Add the jack and Cheddar cheeses, cumin, coriander, and chile powder. Season to taste with salt and pepper.

To assemble the tamales, soak the corn husks in warm water for 10 minutes or until pliable. Bring a pot with a large steamer insert to a boil.

Tear 2 of the husks into 12 strips and set aside. Lay 6 husks on a work surface and distribute the dough evenly between them. Using your fingertips, form the dough into a rectangle, leaving a $1/2$-inch border along the sides of the husks. Spoon the filling into the center of the dough and roll the husk lengthwise over the filling to form a tube shape, enclosing the filling in the dough and completely wrapping the dough in the husk. Tie both ends of the husk with the torn strips. Place the tamales in the steamer, cover tightly, and steam for 15 to 20 minutes. Serve immediately with the sauce on the side.

cilantro, look for supple stems and lively, bright green leaves. Cilantro wilts quickly, so keep it in the refrigerator. It can be stored in the refrigerator for up to one week wrapped in a damp paper towel and sealed in an airtight plastic bag.

Coriander seeds, which were mentioned in early Sanskrit writings and in Egyptian tombs dating back to 960 B.C., do not taste at all like cilantro. The tiny beige seeds are fragrant, spicy, sweet, mild. They are used in baked goods, pickling, and curries to add a bit of sweetness.

Salads, Soups & Sides

Seasonal Greens with Garlic-Cabernet Dressing

SERVES 6

GREENS

Wash greens thoroughly and spin them completely dry in a salad spinner. Their freshness depends on it! Store greens wrapped in a damp paper towel in a plastic bag in the refrigerator.

ARUGULA

We use a lot of arugula at the restaurant because we are fond of its tenderness and nutty, spicy flavor. We use it in everything from salads and sandwiches to pasta, which we toss it into at the last moment. Don't overcook this tender green.

It is surprisingly easy to make salad dressing, and this is a good all-purpose one. Substitute it for the bottled dressing you usually reach for when you're in a hurry. This dressing is also good on grilled potatoes, tossed in a warm spinach salad, or drizzled over grilled tuna. It will keep for weeks in the refrigerator—if you can refrain from using it up as soon as you make it. The cabernet vinegar is more acidic than a regular wine vinegar and has a lush, berrylike flavor. You'll find a good cabernet vinegar in gourmet markets and specialty food shops.

GARLIC-CABERNET DRESSING
2 cloves garlic, chopped
2 shallots, chopped
2 teaspoons Dijon mustard
1/4 cup cabernet vinegar or red wine vinegar
1 head garlic, roasted and squeezed out of papery skin (page 188)
2 teaspoons chopped fresh rosemary
3/4 cup extra virgin olive oil
Salt
Freshly ground black pepper

SALAD
1 head butter lettuce
1 head red leaf lettuce
1 head radicchio
1 small cucumber, peeled and sliced
1 tomato, cut into wedges
1 bunch radishes, sliced
1 red onion, thinly sliced

To prepare the dressing, place the chopped garlic, shallots, Dijon mustard, vinegar, roasted garlic, and rosemary in a small bowl and whisk together. Slowly whisk in the olive oil until the dressing is emulsified and thickened. Season to taste with salt and pepper. Refrigerate until ready to use. (The dressing may be stored in the refrigerator in a tightly covered container for up to 3 weeks.)

To prepare the salad, wash and dry the lettuces, tear the leaves into pieces, and place in a large salad bowl. Add the cucumber, tomato, radishes, and onion and toss well. Add about 1/4 cup of the dressing, or enough to lightly coat the leaves, and toss well to coat evenly.

Transfer the salad to a large salad bowl and serve immediately.

Warm Spinach Salad
with Pancetta & Gorgonzola Dressing

SERVES 4

This salad is easy to make, but timing the assembly right is imperative. You need to have everything ready before you toss the salad—the plates should be at the ready and the guests seated—or the spinach may become overheated and wilt before anyone gets their first forkful. The dressing can even be made up to a week ahead and warmed just before serving.

PANCETTA AND GORGONZOLA DRESSING

1 teaspoon vegetable oil
1/2 cup diced pancetta
1/4 cup sherry vinegar
3 cloves garlic, chopped
2 shallots, chopped
1 tablespoon Dijon mustard
3/4 cup olive oil
1/2 cup Gorgonzola cheese
2 teaspoons cracked black pepper
Salt

1 1/2 pounds fresh spinach (about 2 bunches), cleaned and patted dry
1 cup sliced wild or button mushrooms
1 red onion, sliced
1 red bell pepper, seeded, deribbed, and julienned
1/2 cup hazelnuts, toasted and coarsely chopped (page 192)

To prepare the dressing, put the vegetable oil in a sauté pan and heat over high heat until hot. Add the pancetta and cook until crispy. Transfer the pancetta to paper towels to drain and let the oil cool in the pan. Place the vinegar, garlic, shallots, and mustard in a medium bowl and mix well. Slowly whisk in the olive oil and pancetta oil until the dressing is emulsified and thickened. Stir in the crumbled blue cheese, add the pepper, and season to taste with the salt.

To prepare the salad, place the spinach, mushrooms, onions, and bell peppers in a large metal bowl. Add 2 tablespoons of dressing per person and toss with the greens. Place the metal bowl directly on a burner over high heat. Using a hot pad to hold the bowl, toss the salad on the heat just until it begins to wilt. Divide the salad among 4 dinner plates, top with the toasted hazelnuts, and serve.

MUSTARD GREENS
Tiny, baby mustard greens are good in salads. I also like them sautéed with a little balsamic vinegar, garlic, and salt and pepper. Mustard greens are a great bed for meats, such as pork roast.

SALAD GREENS
We use a combination of tender and bitter wild greens, called mesclun mix. We also make our own green salad mix with baby radicchio, lolla rossa, and other baby lettuces. We use romaine for salads with heavy dressings, like Ceasar salads. We use spinach for salads that should have a lot of body.

Asparagus Salad with Roasted Herbs

SERVES 6

Asparagus is always one of the first vegetables we see in our kitchen at the bistro and it just happens to be one of my favorites, too. This salad is great for those early days of spring when it could be warm and sunny or cold and rainy. To transform it into a great entrée salad, just place a layer of julienned roasted chicken under the goat cheese and serve it with crusty French bread and a glass of Pinot Noir. The dressing can be made 1 week ahead and warmed just before serving.

2 pounds asparagus

DRESSING

1 tablespoon olive oil

2 shallots, chopped

3 cloves garlic, chopped

1 tablespoon mixed chopped fresh herbs
   (such as basil, rosemary, and thyme)

1/4 cup red wine

1/4 cup balsamic vinegar

2/3 cup olive oil

Salt

Cracked black pepper

1/2 pound mesclun mix or mixed
   wild greens

12 ounces soft mild goat cheese,
   crumbled

1/2 cup toasted unseasoned bread
   crumbs

Prepare a large ice water bath. Bring a large stockpot of water to a boil over high heat. Add the asparagus and blanch, about 4 minutes, or until al dente, then transfer to an ice water bath. When cool, drain the asparagus and set aside.

To prepare the dressing, heat the olive oil in a sauté pan over high heat until very hot. Add the shallots and garlic and lightly sauté, just until fragrant, about 1 minute. Add the herbs and sauté until the herbs are fragrant, then add the red wine and reduce until only about 2 tablespoons of wine remain. Add the vinegar and transfer to a medium bowl. Slowly whisk in the olive oil, until the dressing is emulsified and thickened. Season to taste with salt and pepper and set aside.

To prepare the salad, distribute the greens and asparagus among 6 individual plates and drizzle the warm dressing over the top. Sprinkle the goat cheese and bread crumbs over the top and serve.

Chile & Tomato Saifun Noodle Salad

SERVES 4

This is a versatile dish. It makes a great appetizer, main course, or side dish served with grilled fish or prawns. Or, serve slices of pork tenderloin or duck roasted with a spicy pepper sauce on top of the saifun noodles. Sometimes I like to add bean sprouts, fresh peas, and sautéed shiitake mushrooms, or other wild mushrooms. Saifun bean thread noodles have a delightful texture and absorb flavors beautifully. You can make the dish less spicy by holding back on the chile paste. The dressing is red, so using both red and yellow tomatoes adds visual interest. Let the salad sit at room temperature for at least 30 minutes before serving so the noodles can fully absorb the flavors.

1/2 pound saifun (rice stick) noodles

DRESSING

1/4 cup rice vinegar

3 tablespoons sugar

Zest and juice of 1 lime

2 teaspoons chile paste

3 cloves garlic, chopped

2 teaspoons fish sauce

1/4 cup vegetable oil

Soy sauce

2 ripe tomatoes, diced

1 small peeled cucumber, thinly sliced into rounds

2 tablespoons chopped cilantro

2 tablespoons chopped fresh mint

3 to 4 green onions, minced

To prepare the noodles, soak them in a bowl of warm water for about 10 to 15 minutes to soften. Bring 5 cups of water to a boil in a medium saucepan, add the softened noodles, and cook until tender, about 1 minute. Drain the noodles and briefly rinse them under cold running water to stop the cooking process. Drain again and place in the refrigerator to chill.

To prepare the dressing, mix together the vinegar, sugar, zest, juice, and chile paste in a medium bowl. Stir in the garlic and fish sauce. Slowly whisk in the oil until the dressing is emulsified and thickened. Season to taste with the soy sauce and set aside.

To finish the salad, place the chilled noodles in a large bowl. Add the tomatoes, cucumbers, cilantro, mint, and green onions and toss well. Pour the dressing over the salad and toss well to coat evenly. Refrigerate the salad for at least 30 minutes, then serve.

Seared Scallop Salad with Citrus Vinaigrette

SERVES 4

This refreshing seafood salad can be served as either an appetizer or an entrée. Either way, make the dressing ahead of time and set up the plates, then sear the scallops at the very last minute. You want the scallops to be crispy on the outside and meltingly soft when you bite into them. The light citrus vinaigrette has many uses—try it served over blanched asparagus or grilled halibut.

CITRUS FRUITS

Anytime something tastes flat, add a little citrus juice to improve the contrast and depth of flavor. The juice of lemons, limes, and oranges is great for lifting just about every spice. And the acid can make other ingredients, such as chiles, come alive. When buying citrus, look for fruit that are heavy for their size. Their skins should have a deep color and be smooth. Avoid dry-looking or soft fruit. Citrus last several weeks in the refrigerator.

CITRUS VINAIGRETTE
2 cloves garlic, chopped
1 shallot, chopped
2 tablespoons rice vinegar
2 teaspoons orange juice concentrate
2 teaspoons chopped orange zest
1/3 cup extra virgin olive oil
Salt
Cracked black pepper

1 head butter lettuce
4 ounces arugula (about 2 cups)
1/2 small red onion, julienned
2 oranges, peeled and sectioned (page 192)
1 tablespoon olive oil
1 pound sea scallops, rinsed and patted dry

To prepare the vinaigrette, combine the garlic, shallot, vinegar, orange juice concentrate, and zest in a medium bowl. Slowly whisk in the olive oil until the dressing is emulsified and thickened. Season to taste with the salt and pepper.

To prepare the salad, arrange the lettuce and arugula on 4 plates. Arrange the red onions and orange segments on top of the greens. Heat the olive oil in a 10-inch sauté pan over high heat until smoking hot. Add the scallops and sear on both sides just until the scallops are translucent, about 2 minutes.

To serve, distribute the scallops among the salads, placing them on the greens, and drizzle the vinaigrette over the top. Serve immediately.

Quinoa Salad with Fennel & Roasted Shallots

SERVES 4

Quinoa is a delicious grain with a nutty flavor. Look for it in natural foods stores and gourmet markets. Once you've learned to cook it, you'll want to try substituting it for rice and other grains in all kinds of recipes.

1 cup quinoa
2 cups chicken or vegetable stock (pages 184, 185)
6 shallots, halved lengthwise
1 bulb fennel, peeled and julienned
1 tablespoon plus 1/2 cup olive oil
3 tablespoons sherry vinegar
3 cloves garlic, chopped
1 tablespoon chopped fresh fennel greens
1/2 teaspoon dry mustard powder
Salt
Freshly ground black pepper

Preheat the oven to 325°. Rinse the quinoa under cold running water until the water runs clear. Heat the chicken stock in a 3-quart saucepan over high heat until boiling. Add the quinoa and cook until tender and translucent, about 15 minutes. Remove the pan from the heat and let the quinoa sit for about 5 minutes. Transfer to a medium bowl and set aside.

Put the shallots and fennel in a medium ovenproof sauté pan and drizzle with 1 tablespoon of the olive oil. Place the pan in the oven and roast until tender, about 45 minutes. Remove the pan from the oven and set it aside to cool. When the vegetables are cool enough to handle, remove them from the pan and reserve the oil they roasted in. Coarsely chop the shallots and fennel and add them to the bowl with the quinoa. Toss well to combine.

Combine the vinegar, garlic, fennel greens, and mustard in a small bowl and mix well. Slowly whisk in the remaining 1/2 cup olive oil until the dressing is emulsified and thickened. Stir in the reserved roasting oil and season to taste with salt and pepper. Pour the dressing over the quinoa and mix well.

Place the salad on a platter and serve at room temperature.

FENNEL

Fennel is a root vegetable that adds a nice dimension of flavor to fish dishes, soups, and chowders. Small fennel bulbs can be tasty peeled, quartered, braised, and served as a vegetable. I like to buy fennel bulbs with the greens attached so I can tell how fresh they are. The greens also add a stronger fennel flavor to dishes. To keep them fresh, I cut the greens off when I get home from the market and store them in a plastic bag in the refrigerator.

White Bean & Olive Salad

SERVES 4

This salad always makes me think of summer. It's great to take on picnics or to serve on warm summer nights. It can be served as a salad, as a base for grilled fish or grilled lamb chops, or as a garnish for tomato soup. It is a colorful salad with lots of different textures, and it's very healthful, too. Cannellinis are my favorite white beans because they are especially flavorful, but you can use any white beans.

2 cups dried white beans
1 small red onion, julienned
2 plum tomatoes, chopped
3/4 cup chopped pitted cured olives (such as kalamata)
1 bunch arugula, rinsed well and patted dry
1/4 cup sherry vinegar
3 cloves garlic, chopped
2 shallots, chopped
1 tablespoon whole-grain mustard
3/4 cup extra virgin olive oil
Zest of 1 lemon
1 tablespoon chopped fresh basil
1 teaspoon cracked black pepper
Salt

To prepare the salad, soak the white beans overnight. The next day, cook the beans in 2 quarts of boiling water until tender. Drain the beans well, and place them in a medium bowl. Add the onion, tomatoes, olives, and arugula and toss to mix. Set aside.

In a small bowl, mix together the vinegar, garlic, shallots, and mustard. Slowly whisk in the olive oil until emulsified. Add the zest, basil, and pepper and mix well. Season to taste with the salt. Pour the dressing over the bean mixture and refrigerate for at least 30 minutes. Serve cold.

Warm Potato Salad with Apple-Curry Dressing

SERVES 6

We served this salad at a luncheon we catered, and it was an instant hit. There's a lot going on in this salad. You have the spice of the curry and the tang and crunch of the apples contrasting with the smoothness of the potatoes. Sometimes, I also throw in a bit of diced red onion for color. I use yellow Finns but you can also use Yukon golds; both have a buttery color and texture. This salad is especially good warm and it is great with pork.

2 tablespoons olive oil

2 to 3 pounds yellow Finn potatoes, halved if large

1 teaspoon salt

1 teaspoon freshly ground black pepper

APPLE-CURRY DRESSING

1/4 cup rice vinegar

1 tablespoon chopped peeled fresh ginger

2 cloves garlic, chopped

2 shallots, chopped

1 tablespoon curry powder, toasted (page 192)

2 tablespoons sweet hot chile sauce

2/3 cup vegetable oil

Soy sauce

1/2 cup walnuts, toasted (page 191)

2 Granny Smith apples, cored, and sliced

To prepare the potatoes, preheat the oven to 425°. Put the olive oil in a roasting pan and heat it in the oven until smoking hot. Remove the pan from the oven and add the potatoes. Season with salt and pepper. Return the pan to the oven and roast until the potatoes are tender, about 25 minutes. Remove from the oven and season again.

Meanwhile, prepare the dressing. Place the vinegar, ginger, garlic, shallots, and curry powder in a medium bowl and mix well. Add the chile sauce to the mixture and whisk to combine. Slowly whisk in the vegetable oil until the dressing is emulsified and thickened. Season to taste with the soy sauce.

Put the warm potatoes in a large bowl and add the walnuts and apples. Add the dressing and toss well to coat. Serve warm or refrigerate and serve cold.

Potato-Leek Soup with Grilled Chicken

SERVES 6

I know potato-leek soup isn't very glamorous, but it's one of my favorites. And it's a popular Sunday-evening meal at my house. Once you get the soup cooking, you don't have to do much else, which I like after cooking all week. You can add a 1/2 cup or so of wild mushrooms or even roasted peppers to change the flavors.

2 tablespoons unsalted butter
5 leek bulbs, washed thoroughly and julienned
3 cloves garlic, chopped
1 onion, diced
1 1/2 cups dry sherry
5 large potatoes, peeled and diced
6 cups chicken stock (page 184)
1 cup heavy whipping cream
2 tablespoons Durkee's cayenne sauce
1 tablespoon chopped fresh thyme
Salt
Freshly ground black pepper

GRILLED CHICKEN
2 teaspoons olive oil
1 tablespoon chopped fresh basil
1 teaspoon salt
1 teaspoon freshly ground black pepper
4 boneless and skinless chicken breasts

Heat the butter in a large stockpot over high heat until very hot. Add the leeks, garlic, and onion and lightly sauté for about 3 minutes. Add the sherry and reduce over high heat and until about 1/2 cup of liquid remains. Add the potatoes and stock, lower the heat to medium, and cook until the potatoes are tender, 10 to 15 minutes. Purée the soup with a handheld blender or in batches in a food processor or blender and then return the soup to the pan. Add the cream, cayenne sauce, and thyme and season to taste with lots of salt and black pepper. Simmer for about 10 minutes.

Meanwhile, to prepare the chicken, oil the grill rack and preheat the grill. Mix together the olive oil, basil, and salt and pepper in a small bowl and rub the chicken with the mixture. Place the chicken on the hot grill and cook for 2 to 3 minutes on each side. Remove chicken from the grill, let cool for a few minutes, and then julienne it. Add the chicken to the soup and stir. Cook for a few more minutes if the chicken is still pink inside.

Ladle soup into soup bowls and serve hot.

LEEKS

The leek is a mild-mannered cousin of garlic and onions. It looks like a huge green onion, but it is not as spicy. Leeks have a mild, sweet, subtle flavor. When buying leeks, avoid the "big timber" or log-sized ones. Use the white part only; the green part lends a green tinge to dishes. Leeks are great for flavoring stocks and baby leeks are delicious braised.

Leeks are native to the Mediterranean and have been enjoyed for thousands of years. Emperor Nero, during his reign in A.D. 37 to 68, believed that leeks improved his singing voice, so he ate prodi-

Five-Onion Soup

SERVES 6

This is a soup I used to make at a restaurant I worked at before we opened Caprial's. I can't claim to have invented the recipe, but after so many years my own version has definitely evolved. It's creamy, rich and very mild, because the onions cook for so long.

- 2 tablespoons olive oil
- 4 leek bulbs, washed thoroughly and julienned
- 2 yellow onions, julienned
- 2 white onions, julienned
- 2 red onions, julienned
- 4 shallots, coarsely chopped
- 4 cloves garlic, coarsely chopped
- 1 cup dry sherry
- 1 cup brandy
- 6 cups chicken stock or vegetable stock
  (pages 184, 185)
- 1 1/2 cups heavy whipping cream
- 2 tablespoons chopped fresh thyme
- Salt
- Freshly ground black pepper

Heat the olive oil in a large stockpot over high heat until very hot. Add the leeks, onions, and shallots, and cook for 10 to 15 minutes, or until the onions are tender. Add the sherry and brandy and reduce until about 1 cup of liquid remains. Add the stock and simmer for about 1 hour.

Purée the soup with a handheld blender or in batches in the bowl of a food processor or in a blender, and then return the soup to the pan. Add the cream and cook for about 15 minutes more. Add the thyme and season to taste with salt and pepper.

Ladle the soup into soup bowls and serve hot.

gious quantities. A few centuries later, the Welsh made leeks their national symbol because they were convinced the leeks they wore on their helmets strengthened them for battle. Leeks still have many champions in the kitchen.

Leeks need to be cleaned well both inside and outside before using. They are grown in sandy soils, and the soil is piled along the sides of the plant to prevent exposure to the sun as they grow. To clean leeks, cut them in half lengthwise, pull out the woody core, soak them in cold water, and then wash them again to get rid of any sand.

Chicken & Chile Soup

SERVES 6

I finish this soup with a squeeze of lime to cut the heat of the chiles and add lots of cumin, my favorite spice.

2 tablespoons vegetable oil

5 small dried Mexican chiles

1 1/2 cups water plus more as needed

4 ripe tomatoes, halved, seeded, and
    diced (page 190)

1 small onion, diced

4 cloves garlic, chopped

1 quart chicken stock (page 184)

3 boneless and skinless chicken breasts,
    julienned

3 tablespoons masa harina

1 tablespoon chopped cilantro

Minced zest of 2 limes

Juice of 1 lime

Salt

Freshly ground black pepper

1/2 cup sour cream

1 lime, cut into wedges

SHALLOTS

Shallots are related to onions, but they are milder and sweeter. They look more like garlic, with a head composed of several cloves. The skin varies from rose to pale brown and the cream-colored flesh is usually tinged with green or purple. Choose shallots that are plump and firm without wrinkles or sprouts. Refrigerate shallots for up to one week. Store shallots in a cold, dry, well-ventilated place for up to one month.

Heat 1 tablespoon of the vegetable oil in a small sauté pan over high heat until very hot. Add the chiles and cook until fragrant, about 1 minute. Transfer the chiles to a bowl, cover with 1 cup of the water, and set aside for 30 minutes.

Remove the chiles from the water with a slotted spoon and place them on a cutting board. Reserve the soaking liquid. Remove the chile stems and seeds and place the chiles in a blender. Add the reserved soaking liquid and purée until smooth. Add the tomatoes, onion, and garlic and purée.

Place 1 teaspoon of the remaining oil in a large stockpot and heat over high heat until very hot. Add the purée and cook for about 10 minutes, or until thick. Add the chicken stock and simmer uncovered for about 30 minutes.

Meanwhile, heat the remaining 2 teaspoons of oil in a medium sauté pan over high heat until smoking hot. Add the chicken and sauté for 4 to 5 minutes, until just opaque and cooked through. Remove chicken from the pan and set aside. (Refrigerate chicken if waiting longer than 10 minutes to finish recipe.)

Place the masa in a small bowl and add about 1/2 cup of the remaining water. Stir with a whisk until smooth. Whisk the masa mixture into the simmering soup. Add the cilantro, zest, and lime juice. Season to taste with salt and pepper.

Divide the chicken among the soup bowls, then ladle the soup over. Garnish each with a dollop of sour cream and a lime wedge and serve hot.

Wild Rice & Mushroom Soup

SERVES 6

This hearty, satisfying soup achieves its richness through a purée of wild rice and mushrooms. Dry red wine adds depth and a bit of tang. And remember—don't cook with anything you wouldn't drink!

WILD RICE

2 teaspoons olive oil

2 cloves garlic, chopped

1 shallot, chopped

1 cup wild rice

3 cups vegetable or chicken
   stock (page 184,185)

Salt

Freshly ground black pepper

1 tablespoon olive oil

1 onion, diced

3 cloves garlic, chopped

3 cups sliced button mushrooms

3 cups sliced wild mushrooms

2 cups red wine

3 potatoes, peeled and diced

6 cups chicken stock (page 184)

1 cup heavy whipping cream

1 tablespoon chopped fresh rosemary

2 teaspoons chopped fresh thyme

2 tablespoons Durkee's cayenne sauce

Salt

Freshly ground black pepper

To prepare the rice, heat the oil in a saucepan over high heat. Add the garlic and shallot and sauté one minute. Add the rice and sauté 1 to 2 minutes. Add the stock and season to taste with salt and pepper. Cover, decrease the heat to medium-low, and simmer for 20 minutes, or until tender.

Heat the olive oil in a stockpot over high heat until very hot. Add the onion and garlic and lightly sauté for about 2 minutes. Add the mushrooms and sauté until tender, about 5 minutes. Add the red wine and reduce until about $1/2$ cup of liquid remains. Add the potatoes and stock and cook until the potatoes are very tender, 10 to 15 minutes.

Purée the soup with a handheld blender or in batches in the bowl of a food processor or in a blender and then return the soup to the stockpot. Add the cream, rosemary, and thyme and cook for about 15 minutes. Add the rice and cayenne sauce and season to taste with salt and pepper.

Ladle soup into soup bowls and serve hot.

Spicy Roasted Butternut Squash Soup

SERVES 6

As its name suggests, butternut squash is rich, buttery, and slightly nutty tasting. In this velvety smooth soup, the squash mingles with the exotic flavors of ginger and curry. The curry and cumin add warmth in the form of spice. It's one of my favorite recipes in the whole book.

1 large butternut squash, peeled and diced
4 cloves garlic
2 tablespoons olive oil
1 onion, diced
1 tablespoon peeled, chopped fresh ginger
1/2 cup mirin
1/2 cup dry sherry
4 cups chicken stock (page 184)
2 teaspoons chile sauce
2 teaspoons curry powder, toasted (page 192)
1 teaspoon ground toasted cumin seeds (page 192)
Soy sauce
Crème fraîche (page 189)

Preheat the oven to 425°. Place the squash and garlic in a roasting pan and drizzle with 1 tablespoon of the olive oil. Place the pan in the oven and roast until the squash is tender, about 40 minutes.

Heat the remaining tablespoon of olive oil in a stockpot over high heat until hot. Add the onion and ginger and sauté until fragrant. Add the mirin and sherry and reduce to about 1/2 cup, about 4 to 5 minutes. Add the stock, cooked squash, and garlic and cook for 15 to 20 minutes. Add the chile, curry, and cumin and purée with a handheld blender or in batches in the bowl of a food processor or in a blender. Season to taste with soy sauce. Taste for spiciness and adjust, adding more chile sauce if you like it hotter.

Ladle the soup into bowls. Garnish with a dollop of crème fraîche and serve hot.

Grilled Tomato Soup with Gremolata

SERVES 6

The mere mention of tomato soup takes some people back to childhood, when they were home sick from school and it was part of their mothers' prescription for restoring health. If you're one of them, you'll delight in this grown-up tomato soup. It's really important to use the ripest tomatoes because they give the soup its natural sweetness and acidity. The gremolata provides a bit of saltiness that perfectly complements the flavor of the tomatoes.

3 pounds ripe tomatoes, halved and
    seeded (page 190)
2 tablespoons olive oil
3 cloves garlic, chopped
3 shallots, chopped
1 onion, diced
1 1/2 cups red wine
6 cups chicken or vegetable stock
    (pages 184, 185)
1 tablespoon chopped fresh basil
2 teaspoons chopped fresh rosemary
Salt
Freshly ground black pepper

GREMOLATA
3 cloves garlic, minced
Zest of 1 lemon, minced
2 tablespoons chopped flat-leaf
parsley
4 oil- or salt-packed anchovy fillets,
    minced

To prepare the soup, generously oil the grill rack and preheat the grill. Place the seeded tomatoes in a large bowl and toss with 1 tablespoon of the olive oil. Set the tomatoes cut-side down on the grill and grill for about 3 minutes. Remove with a metal spatula and set aside.

Heat the remaining 1 tablespoon olive oil in a large stockpot over high heat until very hot. Add the garlic, shallots, and onion and lightly sauté for about 3 minutes. Add the red wine and reduce until about 1/2 cup liquid remains. Add the grilled tomatoes and stock and simmer for 30 to 45 minutes.

Purée the soup with a handheld blender or in batches in the bowl of a food processor or in a blender and then return the soup to the pan. Add the basil and rosemary and season to taste with salt and pepper. Simmer for another 10 minutes.

Meanwhile, prepare the gremolata, placing all of the ingredients in a small bowl and mixing well.

Ladle the soup into bowls and garnish with a spoonful of gremolata. Serve hot.

Roasted Garlic–Blue Cheese Bisque

SERVES 6

A bisque is a puréed soup that is often thickened with cream. Bisques are usually made with shellfish and have a rich, velvety texture. I created this recipe as a departure from the standard bisque, using garlic as the main flavor instead of shrimp or lobster. This sweet, mellow, creamy soup has a surprising tang (from the blue cheese) and is a perfect, warming winter soup. It is thickened with potatoes and has the lovely underlying flavors of dry sherry and brandy. A dash of cayenne sauce adds just the right amount of zing.

30 whole cloves garlic (about 3 heads), plus 2 cloves, chopped
3/4 cup dry sherry
1/2 cup brandy
5 Yukon gold potatoes, peeled and diced
1 quart chicken stock (page 184)
2 teaspoons Durkee's cayenne sauce
2 cups heavy whipping cream
6 ounces Gorgonzola or other blue cheese
Salt
Freshly ground black pepper
1 tablespoon chopped chives

Heat the oil in a large saucepan over medium-low heat. Add the whole garlic cloves to the pan, decrease the heat to low, and cook until cloves are tender, 10 to 15 minutes. Carefully add the sherry and brandy, increase the heat to high, and reduce the liquid by half, 2 to 3 minutes. Add the diced potatoes and chicken stock and cook until the potatoes are tender. Transfer the soup to a large bowl, add the chopped garlic, and purée with a handheld blender or in batches in the bowl of a food processor or in a blender and then return the soup to the pan. Add the cayenne sauce and cream and cook until the cream comes to a boil. Whisk about 4 ounces of the cheese into the soup. Season to taste with salt and pepper.

Ladle the soup into soup bowls, sprinkle the remaining Gorgonzola and the chives over the bowls, and serve hot.

GARLIC

Garlic has been known for centuries as a miracle food with medicinal as well as culinary value. The ancient Egyptians credited garlic with promoting physical strength and fed it to slaves building the pyramids.

Garlic is a bulb related to leeks, onions, shallots, and chives. Elephant garlic is not actually garlic; it is a member of the leek family and it is too mild for most dishes. Three types of garlic are commonly available: American, which is white-skinned and strong-flavored, and Mexican and Italian, which have mauve

Tortilla Soup

SERVES 6

I know just about everyone has a recipe for this soup, but I just couldn't resist the chance to put my own spin on it. Sometimes I even go a step further and "regionalize" it by adding a handful of Dungeness crabmeat.

TORTILLA STRIPS
1 cup vegetable oil
8 corn tortillas, julienned

SOUP
1 tablespoon olive oil
1 onion, diced
4 cloves garlic, chopped
3 pounds ripe tomatoes, halved, seeded, and diced (page 190)
1/3 cup tomato purée
2 quarts chicken stock (page 184)
1 tablespoon ground toasted cumin seeds (page 192)
2 teaspoons chile powder
2 teaspoons ground toasted coriander seeds (page 192)
2 tablespoons ancho chile powder
2 teaspoons chopped cilantro
Salt
Freshly ground black pepper

1 ripe avocado, peeled and diced
1/2 cup grated sharp Cheddar cheese
1/2 cup sour cream

To prepare the tortilla strips, heat the oil in a 3-quart saucepan over high heat until very hot, about 350°. Fry the tortilla strips in the saucepan in small batches, cooking until crisp. Remove strips with a slotted spoon and transfer to paper towels to drain. Repeat until all strips are fried.

To prepare the soup, heat the olive oil a stockpot until very hot. Add the onion and garlic and sauté for about 3 minutes. Add the tomatoes, toss to mix, and then add the tomato purée. Cook until tomatoes are softened, 3 to 4 minutes. Add the chicken stock, lower the heat to medium, and cook for 1 hour.

Add the cumin, chile powder, coriander, ancho chile powder, and cilantro to the soup and simmer for 15 minutes. Ladle into soup bowls and top each with some of the tortilla strips, avocado, cheese, and sour cream. Serve hot.

skins and mild flavors. Buy garlic often, and in small quantities. Don't buy jarred, chopped garlic; the flavor just isn't good enough. And don't use garlic presses, which waste the precious garlic juice. Nor do I use instant garlic, garlic salt, garlic extract, or bottled garlic juice. I just chop garlic very finely with a chef's knife.

Purchase firm, plump bulbs with dry skins. Avoid heads with shriveled cloves or green sprouts. Store garlic for 3 to 10 days in an open container in a cool, dark place away from other foods that could absorb its odor. Unless otherwise specified, garlic is peeled before it is used.

Smoked Salmon Chowder

SERVES 6

We make this often at the restaurant because my husband, John, makes darn good smoked salmon. I don't thicken this chowder—heavy on top of rich on top of thick just doesn't work. I use a light roux that just coats a spoon and barely thickens the soup; it doesn't compete with the textural interest of the chunks of salmon, potato, and onion. The salmon provides the Northwest touch I always favor. Fresh corn is a good addition; use it when it's in season.

1/2 cup diced pepper bacon (6 to 8 slices)	6 ounces hot-smoked salmon
1 onion, diced	1 teaspoon chopped fresh basil
2 cloves garlic, chopped	1 teaspoon chopped fresh thyme
1 tablespoon olive oil	1 teaspoon chopped fresh marjoram
1/4 cup all-purpose flour	1 tablespoon Durkee's cayenne sauce
1 cup dry sherry	1/2 teaspoon celery salt
1 quart fish stock (page 187)	Salt
4 potatoes, peeled and cut in medium dice	Freshly ground black pepper
2 cups heavy whipping cream	6 sprigs basil or thyme

In a large saucepan or stockpot over medium-low heat, cook the bacon until crispy. Transfer the bacon to a paper towel–lined plate to drain, reserving the drippings in the pan. Add the onion, garlic, and olive oil to the pan and cook over medium heat until the onions are fragrant, about 2 minutes. Gradually add the flour, stirring, and cook for about 1 minute. Slowly whisk in the sherry until combined, and then slowly whisk in the fish stock. Add the potatoes and cook over high heat just until tender, 10 to 15 minutes. Whisk in the cream and add the remaining ingredients, except for the garnish. Bring to a simmer and cook for 10 minutes.

Ladle the soup into soup bowls, garnish with a sprig of basil and serve hot.

Chicken Soup with Noodles & Greens

SERVES 6

This simple, delicious Asian soup is like a stir-fry with a gingery chicken broth. You can use fresh asparagus or savoy cabbage instead of the greens, and linguine or spaghettini can be substituted for the Chinese noodles. To give this recipe some zing, mix a little hot dry Chinese mustard with equal parts of warm water and soy sauce to make a paste. Stir a little of the paste into the soup before serving, or let guests add their own hot paste at the table. Float toasted sesame seeds on top just before serving.

5 cups strong chicken stock (page 184)
2 tablespoons peeled, chopped fresh ginger
4 cloves garlic, chopped
1 stalk lemongrass, cut into 4 pieces
1/2 cup Thai basil or standard basil leaves
3 boneless and skinless chicken breasts, julienned
1/2 small Chinese cabbage, julienned
6 baby bok choy, halved lengthwise
1/4 pound thin Chinese noodles, cooked al dente
1 tablespoon fresh chopped mint
3 to 4 scallions, minced
1 tablespoon sweet, hot chile sauce or other chile paste
Soy sauce
2 tablespoons sesame seeds, toasted (page 192)

Combine the stock, ginger, garlic, lemongrass, and basil in a large stockpot and cook over high heat until flavorful, about 1 hour.

Strain the broth through a fine-meshed strainer and discard the solids. Return the broth to the stockpot. Add the chicken, cabbage, and bok choy and cook over high heat until the chicken is just cooked through and the greens are crisp-tender, about 5 minutes. Add the noodles, mint, scallions, and chile sauce and cook just until the noodles are hot, 3 to 4 minutes. Season to taste with soy sauce.

Ladle the soup into bowls. Sprinkle some sesame seeds over each bowl and serve.

Chilled Mango-Curry Soup

SERVES 6

Chilled soups can be so refreshing on a hot summer day and, to me, superripe mangoes make some of the best cold soups. When selecting mangoes, look for ones with a yellow-pink rosy glow that give a bit when gently pressed. Like most soups, this one improves with time, so prepare it the day before you plan to serve it if possible.

6 ripe mangoes, peeled and diced
2 teaspoons peeled, chopped fresh ginger
2 cloves garlic, chopped
1/2 red onion, diced
1 cup chicken or vegetable stock (pages 184, 185)
2 tablespoons rice vinegar
1 tablespoon curry powder, toasted (page 192)
2 tablespoons sweet, hot chile sauce
    plus additional, as needed
Soy sauce
3 scallions, minced

Put the mangoes, ginger, garlic, and onion in a blender and purée (or purée with a handheld blender). Add the stock, vinegar, curry, and chile sauce and blend just to combine. Season to taste with soy sauce and pour into a medium bowl. Cover with plastic wrap and refrigerate until cold, 1 to 2 hours, or overnight.

Ladle the soup into chilled soup bowls and garnish with some of the scallions, sour cream, and chile sauce. Serve cold.

Grilled Vegetable Shish Kebabs with Sherry-Peppercorn Marinade

SERVES 6

I like to make these shish kebabs in summer for a delicious, colorful side dish or vegetarian entrée. Be sure to use fresh seasonal vegetables, such as blanched potatoes or bell peppers. When you're preparing the vegetables, remember that they will shrink as they cook, so cut them into generous wedges. When grilling vegetables, timing is important. One way to ensure the kebabs will be done at the same time is to put one type of vegetable on each skewer. Another tip is to use onions that taste good raw, like sweet Walla Wallas, because the grilling time is brief and stronger onions can overpower the vegetables. Serve the kebabs with rice or couscous.

2 pounds button mushrooms

1 sweet onion or red onion, cut into chunks

1 small zucchini, cut into chunks

1 small eggplant, cut into chunks

1 yellow squash, cut into chunks

SHERRY-PEPPERCORN MARINADE

1 cup dry sherry

3 cloves garlic, chopped

2 shallots, chopped

1/4 cup sherry vinegar

1 teaspoon green peppercorns

2/3 cup extra virgin olive oil

1 tablespoon chopped fresh thyme

Salt

Freshly ground black pepper

Soak 12 bamboo skewers in a pan filled with water for at least 30 minutes, then dry them with a kitchen towel. Put the vegetables on the skewers and set aside.

To prepare the marinade, combine the sherry, garlic, and shallots in a small sauté pan over high heat and reduce until about 1 tablespoon of the sherry remains. Transfer the sherry mixture to a medium bowl and add the sherry vinegar and peppercorns. Whisk in the olive oil until emulsified. Add the thyme and season to taste with salt and pepper. Pour the marinade over the vegetables and set aside to marinate for at least 30 minutes.

In the meantime, prepare the grill. Place the skewers on the hot grill and cook, occasionally brushing the vegetables with the leftover marinade. Cook for 5 to 8 minutes, or until the vegetables are crisp-tender. Remove skewers from the grill, set on a platter, drizzle with remaining marinade, and serve immediately.

Sautéed Green Beans with Bacon & Garlic

SERVES 4

My grandma used to make a recipe similar to this one, but she always cooked the heck out of the beans. My family and I prefer our beans tender yet crunchy, so I blanch the beans until they are al dente, then shock them in cold water to preserve their color and crispness. I also love crisp bacon, so I cook it until it's completely crisp, and then I cook the onions and garlic in the bacon fat and a splash of dry sherry. I know this technique has fallen out of fashion due to contemporary health concerns, but nothing is better than the aroma of onions and garlic cooking in bacon fat.

- 1 pound fresh green beans
- 1/2 cup diced uncooked bacon (6 to 8 slices)
- 1/2 onion, minced
- 3 cloves garlic, chopped
- 1/4 cup dry sherry
- Pinch of cumin
- 1 teaspoon freshly cracked black pepper
- 1/2 teaspoon salt

Snap off the stem ends of the beans and remove their strings, if any. Fill a large saucepan with water and bring it to a boil. Add the green beans and cook for 3 to 4 minutes to blanch. Drain the beans and put them in a bowl of ice water briefly to stop the cooking process. Drain the beans again, then transfer to a medium bowl and set aside.

In a medium sauté pan, cook the bacon over high heat until crispy. Remove the bacon with a slotted spoon, reserving the bacon drippings, and transfer the bacon to paper towels to drain. Decrease the heat to medium-high. Add the onion and garlic to the pan and sauté until fragrant, about 2 minutes. Add the sherry and cook until about 1 tablespoon of liquid remains. Add the beans, cumin, pepper, salt, and bacon and toss well.

Place the beans on a serving platter and serve immediately.

Oven-Roasted Brussels Sprouts

SERVES 4

This is similar to a recipe we created at the request of *Bon Appetit* magazine for a special Thanksgiving dinner. Roasting brings out the natural sugars and flavors in vegetables and is a simple technique—try substituting your favorites to develop other combinations. When John makes this recipe, he finishes it with a drizzle of lemon-infused olive oil, which is very delicious. To make the lemon oil, bring 2 cups of extra virgin olive oil and the zest of several lemons just to a boil. Remove from the heat, cover, and let rest at room temperature for at least 2 days.

1 tablespoon olive oil

1 onion, julienned

3 cloves garlic, chopped

1 pound Brussels sprouts

2 teaspoons chopped fresh thyme

1 teaspoon freshly cracked black pepper

2 tablespoons sherry vinegar

Salt

Preheat the oven to 350°. Score the bottoms of the sprouts with an **X**. Heat the olive oil in a large ovenproof sauté pan over high heat until smoking hot. Add the onion and garlic and sauté for 1 to 2 minutes, or until fragrant. Add the Brussels sprouts and toss to mix well.

Place the pan in the oven and roast the vegetables for about 10 minutes. Remove the pan from the oven, add the thyme, pepper, and sherry vinegar and return the pan to the oven. Cook until tender, about 5 more minutes. Remove from the oven and season to taste with salt.

Place on a serving platter and serve warm.

Snow Peas Tossed with Ginger & Almonds
SERVES 4

This dish is a good model for experimenting with combining various flavors. I hope you'll stretch the concept and invent variations. You can substitute blanched green beans or English shelling peas for the snow peas, for example, and use cilantro in place of the basil and adjust the amount of chile paste. Or just stick to the recipe; it's simple, and delicious.

> 1 pound snow peas
> 2 teaspoons vegetable oil
> 2 cloves garlic, chopped
> 1 tablespoon peeled, chopped fresh ginger
> 1 teaspoon chile paste or chile sauce
> 1 teaspoon honey
> 2 teaspoons chopped fresh basil plus 4 whole sprigs
> Soy sauce
> 1/2 cup almonds, toasted and chopped
> Pickled ginger

Pinch off the stem ends of the snow peas and remove any strings, if any. Heat the oil in a wok or high-sided large sauté pan over high heat until very hot. Add the garlic and ginger and sauté over high heat until fragrant.

Add the snow peas and toss, stir-frying for about 2 minutes. Add the chile paste, honey, and the 2 teaspoons of basil and cook until the snow peas are crisp-tender, 1 to 2 minutes. Season to taste with the soy sauce, add the almonds, and toss well.

To serve, transfer the snow peas to a serving platter. Garnish with the basil sprigs and pickled ginger, and serve immediately.

GINGER

Ginger is a tropical flowering plant with a spicy, citrusy flavor that chefs have loved for centuries. Its name comes from the Sanskrit and translates as "horny" root because it looks like an antler. Ginger was brought to the Mediteranean from India by the Phoenicians and became a favorite of the Greeks and Romans. Believe it or not, Greek bakers were making gingerbread 2,500 years ago! Ginger is also effective for medicinal purposes. It's a good antidote for motion sickness and indigestion, and it is believed to promote circulation.

Hubbard Squash Purée with Orange & Candied Ginger

SERVES 4

This purée is delicious as a base for pork chops or braised lamb shanks. If you make braised lamb shanks, spoon up that precious wine and herb braising liquid and pour it over the shanks when they're set on the purée; the layers of contrasting flavors, textures, and consistencies are just delicious. You can also make the purée with acorn or butternut squash or serve roasted veggies or grilled fish over it.

- 1 Hubbard squash
- 1/4 cup firmly packed brown sugar
- 1 teaspoon peeled, chopped fresh ginger
- 1 tablespoon chopped candied ginger
- 1 tablespoon orange juice concentrate
- 2 tablespoons unsalted butter
- Salt
- Cracked black pepper
- 1/4 cup hazelnuts, toasted and finely ground (page 192)

Preheat the oven to 425°.

Cut the squash in half lengthwise and place cut-side up on a lightly greased roasting pan. Roast the squash in the oven until tender, about 50 minutes. Remove the squash from the oven. Using a large spoon, scrape the squash flesh into the bowl of a food processor. Add the brown sugar, fresh ginger, candied ginger, orange juice concentrate, and butter and purée until smooth. Season to taste with the salt and pepper.

Top with the ground hazelnuts and serve immediately. To serve refrigerated purée, reheat just until warm through, then top with the ground hazelnuts and serve.

When buying ginger, look for smooth skin. Wrinkled skin indicates that the root is dry and past its prime. Fresh ginger can be stored in the refrigerator for up to two weeks wrapped in a damp paper towel and covered in plastic wrap, or frozen in a airtight bag for up to two months. Freezing softens its texture, but does not affect its flavor. You may also place the ginger in a jar with a tight-fitting lid and cover it with sherry; it will keep for up to one month stored this way. After the ginger has been used, the ginger-infused sherry keeps indefinitely and is delicious in sauces.

Sweet Corn & Pancetta Bread Pudding

SERVES 12

This bread pudding is like stuffing, only better because it's supermoist and flavorful. In a class I taught in Toronto, I made a fish covered with ancho chiles, and served it with this bread pudding on the side and a tomatillo salsa spooned over both. The tangy salsa with the savory pancetta and the sweet corn was absolutely yummy, but it was the bread pudding that really wowed the class. To serve it, cut a wedge as if you were serving cake. I like to use fresh corn kernels, but you could substitute fresh peas or sautéed wild mushrooms. If you can't find pancetta, pepper bacon can be used instead.

1/4 pound pancetta, diced	3 cups half-and-half
1 Walla Walla or other sweet onion, diced	1 tablespoon chopped fresh thyme
4 cloves garlic, chopped	2 teaspoons fresh marjoram
Kernels from 2 ears of corn (about 1 cup)	1/2 teaspoon celery salt
1/4 cup diced dry-packed sundried tomatoes	5 eggs, slightly beaten
	Salt
6 cups cubed French bread	Freshly ground black pepper

Place the pancetta in an ungreased medium sauté pan and cook over medium to high heat until the pancetta is crispy. Transfer pancetta with a slotted spoon to a paper towel to drain, reserving the fat in the pan. Add the onion and garlic to the pan and sauté in the pancetta fat until fragrant, about 2 minutes. Add the corn and lightly sauté for 3 minutes. Add the sundried tomatoes. Remove the pan from the heat and set aside to cool completely.

Preheat the oven to 350°. Butter a 10-inch springform pan. Put the cooled vegetable mixture into a large bowl. Add the bread and toss to mix. In a separate bowl, combine the half-and-half, thyme, marjoram, celery salt, and eggs and mix well. Pour the egg mixture over the French bread and press the bread with your hands or a spatula to help it absorb the liquid. Let the mixture sit for at least 10 minutes and then pour it into the prepared pan. Place the pan in the oven and bake for 50 to 60 minutes, or until a knife inserted in the center comes out clean. Remove the pudding from the oven and let it cool for about 5 minutes.

Cut the pudding into wedges and serve while still warm.

Mashed Celeriac with Mascarpone

SERVES 4

Celeriac, or celery root, is a terrific vegetable that is too often overlooked. It has the same flavor as celery but is milder and has a much better texture. When raw, it is crisp, like daikon. When cooked, it is velvety smooth, more so than potatoes because it does not have as much starch as potatoes. For a dish that is less delicate and has more body, substitute potatoes for half of the celeriac. The mascarpone's rich, slightly sweet flavor is perfect in this dish. In winter we serve braised veal or lamb shanks and on top of this celeriac. It is delicious.

2 large celeriac, peeled and diced
5 whole cloves garlic
8 ounces mascarpone
2 tablespoons unsalted butter
Salt
Freshly ground black pepper

Preheat the oven to 350°. Put the celeriac and garlic in a large saucepan and cover with water. Simmer over high heat until the celeriac is tender, about 15 minutes. Drain the celeriac and garlic and place them on a baking sheet.

Bake the celeriac and garlic for about 10 minutes to dry them. Remove from the oven, return to the saucepan, and mash well with a potato masher. Add the mascarpone and butter and mix thoroughly. Season to taste with salt and pepper and serve warm.

Spicy Coconut Jasmine Rice

SERVES 4

This is a perfect side dish with any Asian-inspired dinner, but it is also a good partner for grilled fish or beef tenderloin. If you prefer, you can substitute basmati rice—both are fragrant and have a wonderful toasty flavor.

2 teaspoons vegetable oil
2 cloves garlic, chopped
1 tablespoon peeled, chopped fresh ginger
2 shallots, chopped
1 teaspoon chile paste
1 cup jasmine or basmati rice, rinsed
1 1/3 cups chicken or vegetable stock (pages 184, 185)
1 cup coconut milk
1 teaspoon chopped fresh basil
1 tablespoon instant sour paste (optional)
Salt
Freshly ground black pepper

Preheat the over to 350°.

Heat the oil in a medium ovenproof saucepan until very hot. Add the garlic, ginger, and shallots and lightly sauté over medium heat, about 2 minutes. Add the chile paste and rice and toss. Add the stock and coconut milk, increase the heat to high, and bring to a boil. Stir in the basil and sour paste, and season to taste with salt and pepper.

Cover the saucepan, place it in the oven, and cook for 15 minutes. Remove the pan from the oven, stir the rice, and return to the oven to cook for another 15 minutes, or until the rice is tender. Remove the pan from the oven, fluff the rice with a fork, and taste for spiciness. Stir in more chile paste if you like it spicier.

Place the rice on a serving platter and serve warm.

RICE

Next to wheat, rice is the most important crop in the world. I prefer **jasmine** or **basmati** over long-grain white rice. All rice should be rinsed before cooking to remove the starch. I like to cook rice in stock instead of water because it gives the cooked rice more flavor. **Arborio,** used for risotto, is a starchy, short-grained rice. When you stir it, the starch breaks down and creates risotto's creamy texture. **Wild rice** is a seed of an aquatic plant that is native to the Great Lakes area. It is one of the most costly rices because it is difficult to grow and harvest. Wild rice has a nutty flavor and coarse texture.

Seasoned Mashed Baked Potatoes

SERVES 4

We often fix these mashed potatoes at home. This recipe is especially great for Thanksgiving or other holiday dinners, because you can make it ahead and rewarm it in the oven after your guests arrive. Prepared this way, the potatoes are spicy and have layers of flavor. While they bake, a slightly crisp layer forms on top, providing a satisfying contrast to the creamy potatoes under that "crust."

> 3 pounds Yukon gold potatoes, peeled and diced
> 3/4 cup heavy whipping cream
> 1 tablespoon Dijon mustard
> 2 Anaheim chiles, roasted, peeled, stemmed, seeded, and diced (page 190)
> 1 chipotle pepper, including seeds, stemmed and diced
> 2 teaspoons olive oil
> 1 small onion, minced
> 3 cloves garlic, chopped
> 2 teaspoons ground cumin
> 2 tablespoons unsalted butter
> Salt
> Freshly ground black pepper

Place the potatoes in a medium saucepan, cover with cold water, and bring to a boil. Cook until tender when pierced with a fork, 10 to 15 minutes.

Preheat the oven to 375°. Drain the potatoes and place them on a baking sheet. Place the pan in the oven and bake for about 10 minutes to dry the potatoes. Remove the potatoes from the oven and transfer them to a large bowl. Add the cream and, using a potato masher, mash the cream with the potatoes. Add the mustard, and chiles and mix well. Set aside.

In a small sauté pan, heat the olive oil over high heat until very hot. Add the onion and garlic and lightly sauté for 2 to 3 minutes. Add the cumin and cook with the onions until fragrant, about 1 minute. Add the onion mixture to the potatoes and mix well. Stir in the butter and season to taste with the salt and pepper. (The dish can be made up this point and refrigerated in a covered container until ready to serve.) Place mashed potatoes in a 2-quart casserole and bake in the oven until hot, about 30 minutes. Serve warm.

Cauliflower with Tahini-Yogurt Sauce

SERVES 4

I got the idea for this recipe from a Middle Eastern restaurant in Seattle. We've made some changes to the dish to make it healthier and more flavorful: We steam the cauliflower instead of deep-frying it in a batter; we add herbs and lemon zest, lemongrass, a fragrant lemon tea, or anything that will infuse more flavor into the cauliflower; and we drizzle the tahini sauce over the steamed cauliflower. The sauce is also good on crudités, sandwiches, grilled pork, and any cut of lamb.

1 cauliflower, cut into florets

TAHINI-YOGURT SAUCE
1/2 cup plain yogurt
1/4 cup tahini
2 cloves garlic, chopped
2 teaspoons ground toasted cumin seeds (page 192)
1 teaspoon ground toasted coriander seeds (page 192)
1 teaspoon freshly squeezed lemon juice
Salt
Freshly ground black pepper

To prepare the cauliflower, in a large saucepan, heat 6 cups of salted water to a rolling boil. Add the cauliflower and cook until crisp-tender, 3 to 5 minutes, depending on the size of the cauliflower. Drain the cauliflower and set aside.

To prepare the sauce, combined the yogurt and tahini in a small bowl and mix well. Add the garlic, cumin, coriander, and lemon juice. Season to taste with salt and pepper. Place the cauliflower on a large plate. Drizzle with the sauce and serve warm.

Seared Balsamic-Glazed Carrots

SERVES 4

Carrots are a great side dish. They are delicious, add color to any meal, and almost everybody likes them. I slice the carrots very thinly on the diagonal and sear them at a high heat, which caramelizes their natural sugars. When the carrots are almost done, I add the basalmic vinegar, red wine, and a little garlic and let that reduce. When balsamic vinegar reduces it becomes wonderfully syrupy and thick. If you want to use baby carrots you have to blanch them first. And let them sit for about 30 seconds before tossing when you first put them in the hot oil, or they will never caramelize properly. Also, use pure olive oil, not extra virgin (see pages 88–89).

- 4 peeled carrots, cut thinly on the diagonal
- 2 teaspoons olive oil
- 2 cloves garlic, chopped
- 2 shallots, chopped
- 1/4 cup aged balsamic vinegar
- 1 teaspoon chopped fresh marjoram
- Salt
- Freshly ground black pepper

In a large saucepan, bring about 1 quart of salted water to a boil. Add the carrots, blanch for about 2 minutes, and drain. Heat the olive oil in a large sauté pan over high heat until smoking hot. Add the carrots and allow them to sit in the pan to sear, 2 to 5 minutes or until brown. Toss the carrots and sear again. Add the garlic and shallots and briefly sauté. Add the balsamic vinegar and reduce over high heat until thick and carrots are coated, about 2 minutes. Add the marjoram and season to taste with salt and pepper. Serve piping hot.

Entrées

Roasted Garlic–Stuffed Leg of Lamb with Kalamata Olive Sauce

SERVES 6

ROSEMARY

Rosemary is an herb that grows wild on the Mediterranean coasts, and therefore has been a part of Western culture for many years. "Rosemary for remembrance" is an ancient adage that inspired Greeks and Romans to wear rosemary garlands. When this evergreen shrub grew vigorously in a family's garden, it was said that a woman ran the household. Herbal physicians have used rosemary for depression, headaches, and muscle spasms. Rosemary is easy to grow and needs little care. I rarely water ours, and it is still happy and healthy! Plant rosemary in full

Lamb is my favorite meat. I think it has more flavor than beef. I like to slice the meat thinly for an especially nice presentation. If I'm using a round serving tray, I place the slices in a spiral; if the tray is rectangular, I serve the slices in a long line. This is a great dish for early spring.

1 (3- to 4-pound) boneless leg of lamb
3 heads roasted garlic (page 188)
2 teaspoons chopped fresh rosemary
1 teaspoon chopped fresh thyme
1 teaspoon cracked black pepper

KALAMATA SAUCE
2 shallots, chopped
3 cloves garlic, chopped
1 cup red wine
1 quart strong beef or lamb stock (page 186)
1/2 cup pitted kalamata olives, coarsely chopped
1 teaspoon balsamic vinegar
Salt
Freshly ground black pepper

1 tablespoon olive oil
Kosher salt

To prepare the lamb, remove all the fat and silver skin from the leg. Roll the meat out on a cutting board. Place the roasted garlic in a small bowl and mash it into a paste using a fork or wooden spoon. Spread the paste on the inside of the meat and sprinkle the rosemary, thyme, and black pepper over the garlic. Roll the meat jelly-roll style and secure with bucher's twine. Set the lamb on a large plate and place it in the refrigerator. Preheat the oven to 300°.

To prepare the sauce, combine the shallots, garlic, and red wine in a medium saucepan and reduce over high heat until about $1/2$ cup remains. Add the stock and reduce again over medium-high heat until about $1 1/2$ cups remain, 15 to 20 minutes. When the sauce is reduced, add olives to the pan and cook over medium heat for about 15 minutes. Add the vinegar and season to taste with salt and pepper. Keep warm until ready to use.

Heat the olive oil in a large ovenproof sauté pan or roasting pan over high heat until smoking hot. Remove the lamb from the refrigerator and season it with the kosher salt. Place the lamb in the pan and sear all over, 2 to 3 minutes per side. Place the pan in the oven and cook until medium-rare, about 50 minutes.

Remove the lamb from the oven and let it rest for about 3 minutes before slicing. Using a sharp carving knife, slice the meat about $1/8$ inch thick. Place the slices on a serving platter and spoon some of the warm sauce over the top. Serve hot with the remaining sauce on the side.

sun and you will have enough for cooking most of the year. The whole sprig can be frozen, and the leaves can be removed easily by running your thumb and index finger down the branch. I wrap my rosemary in a damp paper towel, then in plastic wrap, and store it for up to 1 week in the refrigerator. To preserve rosemary, hang it upside down in a cool, dark place until it is dry, and then store it in an airtight container for up to 1 year. Rosemary has a strong, almost piney flavor, so use it with care. It is delicious with grilled meats (especially lamb), pork, chicken, fish, potatoes, vegetables, and fruit.

Pepper-Encrusted Salmon with Green Sauce

SERVES 6

After growing up eating wild salmon, I can't get terribly excited about the farmed variety. My favorite is still wild Copper River salmon, which has such a good flavor that it can stand up to all the pepper and the sauce in this recipe. The sauce can be kept in the refrigerator for up to a week. If you prefer, you can grill the salmon after dredging it in the pepper.

GREEN SAUCE

1 bunch fresh parsley, coarsely chopped

1 bunch fresh basil, coarsely chopped

1 tablespoon coarsely chopped fresh mint

4 cloves garlic, chopped

2 heaping tablespoons chopped capers

4 oil- or salt-packed anchovies, chopped

Zest of 1 lemon

2 tablespoons freshly squeezed
   lemon juice

2/3 cup extra virgin olive oil

Salt

Freshly ground black pepper

6 (6-ounce) salmon fillets

1 tablespoon cracked black peppercorns

1 tablespoon cracked green peppercorns

1 tablespoon cracked pink peppercorns

Kosher salt

1 tablespoon extra virgin olive oil
   or vegetable oil

To prepare the sauce, combine the parsley, basil, and mint in a large bowl. Add the garlic, capers, anchovies, lemon zest, and lemon juice and whisk to combine. Slowly whisk in the olive oil and season to taste with salt and pepper. Set aside. (If not using right away, cover and refrigerate. Bring the sauce to room temperature at least 20 to 30 minutes before using.)

To prepare the salmon, preheat the oven to 350°. Combine the black, green, and pink peppercorns in a small bowl. Season the salmon with the kosher salt and coat with the peppercorn mixture. Heat the olive oil in a very large ovenproof sauté pan over high heat until smoking hot. Add the salmon fillets and sear both sides well, about 2 minutes. Put the pan in the oven and bake for 5 to 7 minutes, depending on the thickness of the fillets. To test for doneness, insert a skewer in the fish, then remove it and touch the tip to your lip; if it is warm, the fish is done. Alternatively, grill fillets on a hot grill for about 4 minutes on each side. Remove the pan from the oven and place the fish on a serving platter. Spoon the sauce over the top of each piece of salmon and serve hot.

Hot-As-Hell Chicken on Chinese Noodles with Peanut Sauce

SERVES 4

This is one of our favorite spicy dishes—perfect for cloudy Northwestern days. We initially named and renamed it several times because customers would always ask if it was hot or order it without expecting such spiciness. Finally, I wrote "HOT AS HELL!" on our menu board, and the name stuck. Now we can't take it off the menu without our customers protesting. The yummy peanut sauce is also great with grilled prawns or fish. Leftover peanut sauce will keep for up to 2 weeks in the refrigerator.

PEANUT SAUCE

2 teaspoons peeled, chopped fresh ginger

2 teaspoons chopped cilantro

2 cloves garlic

2 fresh jalapeño peppers

1/2 cup red wine vinegar

1/2 cup soy sauce

1 heaping cup creamy peanut butter

2 teaspoons curry powder, toasted (192)

1/4 cup honey

2 teaspoons dark sesame oil

1 tablespoon olive oil

4 (6-ounce) chicken breast halves

1/2 cup dry sherry

1 cup sweet hot chile sauce

1/2 pound dried Chinese egg noodles, cooked al dente and tossed with a dash of vegetable oil

1/2 cup dry-roasted peanuts or cashews

3 to 4 green onions, minced

To prepare the peanut sauce, combine the ginger, cilantro, garlic, jalapeños, vinegar, soy sauce, and peanut butter in the bowl of a food processor and process until smooth. Scrape down the sides of the bowl and add the curry powder, honey, and sesame oil; process until smooth. Set aside.

Meanwhile, in a very large sauté pan, heat the oil over high heat until smoking hot. Put the chicken breasts in the pan and brown them well, about 2 minutes on each side. Decrease the heat to medium and cook for another 2 to 3 minutes. Add the sherry, increase the heat to high, and cook until about half of the sherry remains, 2 to 3 minutes. Add the chile sauce and turn the breasts to coat them well. Decrease the heat to low and slowly simmer while you prepare the noodles.

continued

Hot-As-Hell Chicken *continued*

Put the noodles in the pasta insert and set in the pot of boiling water or in the stockpot and cook for about 2 minutes to heat through. Strain the cooked noodles and place in a large bowl. Toss them with $1/2$ cup of the peanut sauce and place on a serving platter. Remove the chicken breasts from the sauce and slice. Place the chicken slices on the noodles and pour some of the remaining sauce over the top. Sprinkle with the roasted peanuts and scallions. Serve hot.

Risotto with Caramelized Pumpkin & Chorizo

SERVES 4

Risotto is the ultimate one-pot meal—satisfying and simple, yet special. It comes together in about 30 minutes and you can transform it into a different dish entirely just by adding other vegetables and meats in place of the pumpkin and sausage in this recipe.

1 tablespoon olive oil

2 cups diced peeled pumpkin

1 small onion, diced

2 cloves garlic, chopped

2 cups arborio rice

6 cups chicken stock, heated (page 184)

1 pound chorizo sausage

1 tablespoon chopped fresh marjoram

2/3 cup freshly grated Parmesan cheese or aged goat cheese

Salt

Freshly ground black pepper

Heat the olive oil in a 10-inch, high-sided sauté pan over high heat until smoking hot. Add the pumpkin and cook until caramelized, 4 to 5 minutes. Add the onion and garlic and lightly sauté for about 2 minutes. Add the rice and sauté to toast, 1 to 2 minutes. Add enough of the stock to cover the rice and cook, stirring constantly. When the stock has been absorbed, about 5 minutes, add more hot stock and repeat the process, cooking until the rice is very al dente, about 20 minutes.

Meanwhile, heat a 10-inch sauté pan over high heat. Add the chorizo and cook until just cooked through, 4 to 6 minutes. Drain and discard the fat from the chorizo and add the meat to the risotto. Add the marjoram and $1/3$ cup of the cheese and mix well. Season to taste with the salt and pepper. Divide the risotto among individual plates and top with the remaining grated cheese. Serve hot.

Pan-Seared Halibut with Lemon-Garlic Vin Blanc

SERVES 4

COOKING WINES

Always avoid wines that are considered or labeled as "cooking wines." Good cooking wines don't have to be expensive, just good enough to drink.

MIRIN

Mirin is a very sweet Japanese rice wine made from glutinous rice. It has a low alcohol content. I use it in Asian cooking when I want a hint of sweetness.

PORT

Port is good in certain sauces for beef or pork or for braising dishes that need the rich flavor.

RED WINE

Use a Cabernet, Merlot, or Zinfandel when a

We developed this simple vin blanc sauce for a cooking class. I have added lemon and garlic to the basic sauce. I like to use it with this halibut because there are so many flavors going on in the herb crust. I use halibut, but you could use ling cod, rock cod, or any firm, white-fleshed fish that looks good at the market. The sauce is flexible: you can add different ingredients, such as roasted bell peppers or fresh herbs, and drizzle it over grilled chicken, for example.

VIN BLANC
3/4 cup dry sherry
3 cloves garlic, chopped
2 shallots, chopped
1 cup heavy whipping cream
1 head roasted garlic, cloves squeezed out and chopped
Zest of 1 lemon
2 teaspoons freshly squeezed lemon juice
Salt
Freshly ground black pepper

4 (6-ounce) halibut fillets
Salt
Freshly ground black pepper
1 teaspoon coarsely chopped fresh basil
1 teaspoon coarsely chopped fresh thyme
1 teaspoon coarsely chopped fresh rosemary
1 teaspoon coarsely chopped fresh marjoram
1 tablespoon olive oil
Zest of 1 lemon
1 bunch fresh basil, thyme, or rosemary

To prepare the sauce, combine the sherry, garlic, and shallots in a saucepan and reduce over high heat until about $1/4$ cup of liquid remains. Add the cream and slowly reduce over medium-low heat until about $1/2$ cup of liquid remains. Add the roasted garlic, lemon zest, and lemon juice, and season to taste with salt and pepper. Keep warm until ready to serve.

To prepare the fish, preheat the oven to 350°. Season the fillets with salt and pepper. On a plate, combine the herbs and dredge the fish in the herb mixture. Heat the olive oil in a large ovenproof sauté pan over high heat until smoking hot. Place the fish in the pan and sear well on both sides, 2 to 5 minutes. Place the pan in the oven for 5 to 7 minutes, depending on the thickness of the fillets. To test for doneness, insert a skewer into the center of the fish, then remove it and place the end on your lip; if it is warm, the fish is done. Spoon some of the sauce onto the center of individual plates, and place the halibut on top of the sauce. Garnish with the lemon zest and fresh herbs and serve hot.

recipe calls for red wine. You could even use a red table wine (a blend of varietals) if it is from a reliable vintner.

SHERRY

I often use dry sherry because it adds a nice nutty flavor to dishes. Use a good, dry Spanish sherry, and steer away from cream sherry because it's too sweet.

WHITE WINE

If a recipe calls for a sweet wine, use a Riesling. If it calls for a dry wine, use a Sauvignon Blanc, Fumé Blanc, or a blend. Chardonnay would be my last choice because it is often aged longer in oak, which can make it taste sweeter than other white wines.

Sautéed Salmon with Black Bean–Shrimp Salsa

SERVES 6

The idea for this dish came from a phone call I got from my producer, Chuck Stewart, who lives near San Francisco. He was raving about the sautéed trout, mashed potatoes, and seafood broth he'd had at a local restaurant. I started with that concept and put my own Northwest spin on it. Salmon has enough body to stand up to the spiciness of this salsa and the richness of the shrimp broth. If you substitute another kind of fish, choose another meaty variety, such as tuna, and be careful not to overcook it. The broth takes a little time to make, but also makes a great base for other sauces. Just add cream or reduce the broth and serve it over your favorite fish. This is an especially pretty dish.

BLACK BEAN–SHRIMP SALSA

1 cup cooked black beans

1/2 pound (16 to 20) cooked shrimp, diced

1 small red onion, diced

2 red bell peppers, roasted, peeled, seeded, and diced (page 190)

2 cloves garlic, chopped

2 fresh jalapeño peppers, diced

1 tablespoon chopped fresh basil

1 teaspoon ground cumin

1 teaspoon chile powder

Juice of 1 lemon

2 tablespoons rice vinegar

1/4 cup extra virgin olive oil

Salt

Freshly ground black pepper

SEAFOOD BROTH

3 cloves garlic, chopped

2 shallots, diced

1/2 cup dry white wine

2 1/2 cups seafood stock (page 188)

1 tablespoon unsalted butter

Salt

Freshly ground black pepper

6 (6-ounce) salmon fillets

Salt

Freshly ground black pepper

1/2 cup all-purpose flour

1 1/2 tablespoons olive oil

Fresh basil leaves, minced

2 tablespoons diced red bell pepper

2 tablespoons diced yellow bell pepper

To prepare the salsa, place the black beans, cooked shrimp, onion, roasted red bell peppers, garlic, and jalapeños in a medium bowl and toss well to mix. In a small bowl, combine the basil, ground cumin, chile powder, lemon juice, and rice vinegar and mix well. Whisk in the olive oil and salt and pepper, then pour over the bean mixture. Toss thoroughly and set aside to rest at room temperature for at least 30 minutes.

To prepare the broth, place the garlic, shallots, and wine in a small saucepan and reduce by about half over high heat, 3 to 4 minutes. Add the stock and reduce again by half over medium-high heat, 8 to 10 minutes. Add the butter and season to taste with salt and pepper. Keep warm until ready to use.

To prepare the salmon, season the fillets with salt and pepper. Put the flour on a plate and dredge the fillets in the flour. Pat the fillets gently to remove excess flour. Place the olive oil in a large sauté pan over high heat and heat until smoking hot. Place the salmon in the pan and sear well on both sides, about 3 minutes. If the fish is thicker than $1/2$ inch, bake in a preheated 350° oven for another 4 to 5 minutes.

To serve, place the salmon fillets in individual large, shallow soup bowls. Top with a spoonful of the salsa and ladle about $1/4$ cup of seafood broth over the fillets. Sprinkle the fresh basil and diced bell peppers over the bowls and serve hot.

Pork Tenderloin with Apple Chutney

SERVES 4

Everyone should have a good pork tenderloin recipe in their repertoire—it's one of those low-maintanance meals that always looks so impressive. Pork's firm texture and mild flavor are the perfect match for soft, sweet, tart fruit compotes and chutneys. I'm partial to this one because it showcases our world-famous apples.

APPLE CHUTNEY
2 teaspoons olive oil
1 red onion, julienned
3 cloves garlic, chopped
1/2 cup apple cider
1 tablespoon brown sugar
2 tablespoons sherry vinegar
3 Granny Smith apples, peeled, cored, and sliced
2 teaspoons chopped fresh thyme
1 teaspoon chopped fresh marjoram
1 teaspoon crushed green peppercorns
Salt

1 pork tenderloin (about 2 pounds)
2 teaspoons dried thyme
Salt
Cracked black pepper
1 tablespoon olive oil
1/2 red apple
1 tablespoon fresh thyme leaves

APPLES

Apple trees are one of the oldest and most widely cultivated fruit trees. Granny Smiths are my favorite variety. They are good for baking and for almost any dish that requires cooked apples. They hold up well when cooked. They are also good chopped and added to salads. Granny Smiths are readily available in fall and winter and have good body and tartness. These apples like humid conditions. Store them in the refrigerator crisper for a couple of weeks.

To prepare the chutney, heat the olive oil in a large sauté pan over high heat until very hot. Add the onion and garlic and sauté until fragrant, about 1 minute. Add the cider and brown sugar and bring to a boil. Add the vinegar and sliced apples and cook over high heat until the apples are tender. Add the thyme, marjoram, and peppercorns and cook for 2 to 3 minutes. Season to taste with salt. Keep warm while the tenderloin is cooking (if longer than 20 minutes, gently rewarm before serving).

To prepare the tenderloin, preheat the oven to 350°. Trim the fat from the tenderloin. Rub the meat with the thyme and salt and pepper. Put the olive oil in a large ovenproof sauté pan and heat on high heat until smoking hot. Add the pork to the pan and sear on both sides, about 2 minutes per side. Place the pork in the oven and cook for 10 to 12 minutes (for medium doneness), or until the meat reaches an internal temperature of 145° (use an instant-read meat thermometer to test). Remove the pork from the oven and let it rest for about 2 minutes before slicing.

Using a sharp carving knife, slice the pork 1/4 inch thick on the diagonal. Fan out about 5 slices on each individual plate. Place a generous spoonful of the chutney over the tenderloin. Cut the apple half into thin slices. Garnish the plates with the apple slices and fresh herbs. Serve hot.

Rack of Lamb with Horseradish Crust & Red Wine Jus Lié

SERVES 4

This lamb has a delicious crust of horseradish, fresh herbs, bread crumbs, lots of garlic, and a little rosemary. I prefer fresh horseradish. The root will keep in your refrigerator forever, and it's good for those times when nothing else will do. You can, however, use prepared horseradish; just be sure to get one without added chemicals and preservatives.

The sauce, a jus lié (pronounced Joo-lee-ay), is au jus with a little thickening. It's a simple sauce, similar to a sauce of thickened pan drippings. You can substitute veal or beef stock if you don't have lamb stock on hand.

2 racks of lamb (about 14 bones), trimmed
Salt
Freshly ground black pepper
2 teaspoons olive oil

HORSERADISH CRUST

1 tablespoon Dijon mustard

1 clove garlic, chopped

1 tablespoon chopped fresh or prepared horseradish

1 teaspoon extra virgin olive oil

1 tablespoon chopped fresh thyme

1/4 cup breadcrumbs

RED WINE JUS LIÉ

2 cups dry red wine

2 shallots, chopped

3 cloves garlic, chopped

3 cups rich lamb or veal stock (page 186)

1 teaspoon cornstarch

1 teaspoon unsalted butter

Salt
Freshly ground black pepper

Preheat the oven to 350°.

To prepare the lamb, season the meat with salt and pepper. Heat the oil over high heat in a very large sauté pan. Add the lamb and sear it well, 2 to 3 minutes. Remove the lamb from the pan and set it aside to cool.

To prepare the crust, place all of the ingredients in a medium bowl and mix well.

Using your fingers, press the crust onto the meat side of the rack. Place the coated meat in a roasting pan and roast in the oven for about 15 minutes for medium-rare to medium doneness. Meanwhile, make the sauce.

To prepare the sauce, place the wine, shallots, and garlic in a medium saucepan and reduce over high heat until about $1/4$ cup of the red wine remains. Add the stock and reduce until about $3/4$ cup of liquid remains. Bring the sauce to a boil. Put the cornstarch in a small bowl and add just enough water to soften it. Whisk the cornstarch into the boiling sauce. Add the butter and season to taste with salt and pepper.

Remove the lamb from the oven and let the meat rest for about 2 to 3 minutes before slicing. To serve, cut the rack of lamb into individual chops, slicing between the bones. Serve warm with red wine sauce spooned over the top.

Baby Back Ribs
with a Sweet & Spicy Chile Glaze

SERVES 4

In summer, we make ribs once a week at home. John makes great ribs. Friends beg John to make ribs. His secret is cooking them slowly at a low temperature before adding any sauce so they become tender and their natural flavors fully develop. The glaze will keep for up to several months and can be used throughout the summer for steaks, pork, and tuna, as well as ribs.

CHILE GLAZE
1 tablespoon vegetable oil
1 small onion, minced
3 cloves garlic, chopped
1 tablespoon peeled, chopped fresh ginger
1 cup mirin wine
1/4 cup honey
1/2 cup hoisin sauce
1/2 cup tomato purée
1/4 cup fermented black beans
2 teaspoons chile paste
2 tablespoons rice vinegar
Soy sauce

4 pounds baby back ribs
Salt
Freshly ground black pepper

To prepare the glaze, heat the vegetable oil in a large saucepan over high heat until very hot. Add the onion, garlic, and ginger and lightly sauté for 2 to 3 minutes. Add the mirin and reduce over high heat until about $1/4$ cup remains. Add the honey, hoisin, tomato purée, fermented black beans, chile paste, and vinegar and cook until thickened, about 10 minutes. Season to taste with the soy sauce. Put the glaze in a container with a tight-fitting lid and refrigerate until ready to use.

To prepare the ribs, heat a grill until very hot, placing the charcoal under only one half of the barbecue. (If using a gas grill, preheat only one side on high.) Season the ribs with salt and pepper and place them on the side of the grill that is not over coals or not heated). Cook, covered, for about 2 hours.

After the ribs have cooked for two hours, generously brush them with the glaze and place on the side of the grill with the coals. Grill for 20 to 30 minutes, basting them frequently. If the ribs start to brown too much, move them to the cooler side of the grill. When the ribs are very tender, remove them from the grill, place on a cutting board, and cut into portions. Serve with the remaining glaze on the side.

Braised Chicken Curry with Gingered Couscous

SERVES 4

Braising is one of my favorite ways to add flavor and make everyday food like chicken special. This braising liquid is also great with veal shanks. If you want the curry very spicy, use a Thai curry paste. If you want something more moderate, choose a Madrasi curry. (Both are available at gourmet groceries and Asian markets.) Serve this with sautéed vegetables, such as carrots or snow peas.

1 (3- to 4-pound) roasting chicken, cut into pieces
Salt
Freshly ground black pepper
1/2 cup all-purpose flour
1 tablespoon olive oil
1 small onion, diced
3 cloves garlic, chopped
2 shallots, chopped
1 tablespoon peeled, chopped fresh ginger
1/2 cup dry sherry
1/2 cup apple cider
2 cups chicken stock (page 184)
1 tablespoon curry, toasted (page 192)
2 teaspoons chopped fresh basil
1 teaspoon chile paste

GINGERED COUSCOUS

3 cups chicken or vegetable stock (pages 184, 185)
1 tablespoon peeled, chopped fresh ginger
2 cloves garlic, chopped
1 teaspoon ground toasted cumin seeds (page 192)
1/2 teaspoon salt
1/2 teaspoon freshly ground black pepper
1 1/2 cups uncooked couscous
1 teaspoon unsalted butter

4 sprigs basil

To prepare the chicken, preheat the oven to 350°. Season the chicken pieces with the salt and pepper. Put the flour on a large plate and dredge the chicken pieces thoroughly in the flour. Tap the pieces gently to remove any excess flour. Heat the olive oil in a large, ovenproof sauté pan over high heat until smoking hot. Add the chicken pieces and brown well on both sides, 2 to 3 minutes. Add the onion, garlic, shallots, and ginger and sauté lightly for about 2 minutes. Add the sherry and apple cider and cook over high heat until reduced by about half. Add the stock, curry, basil, and chile paste and bring to a boil. Cover the pan with a lid and place it in the oven. Braise for 20 to 30 minutes, or until tender.

Remove the chicken from the pan and transfer to a large plate. Reserve the braising liquid in the pan for the sauce. Reduce the liquid slightly over high heat to thicken, about 5 minutes.

To prepare the couscous, bring the stock to a boil in a 3-quart saucepan. Combine the ginger, garlic, cumin, salt, and pepper in a large mixing bowl. Add the couscous, pour the hot stock over it, and cover the bowl. Let the couscous stand for about 10 minutes, or until all of the liquid is absorbed. Remove the cover, add the butter, and fluff with a fork. Adjust seasoning if desired.

To serve, place the couscous on a large serving platter and top with the chicken pieces. Spoon the sauce over the top and garnish with the basil. Serve hot.

New York Steak with Pepper Coulis & Caramelized Onions

SERVES 4

The onions have a mellow sweetness that contrasts beautifully with the tanginess of the pepper coulis. The colors, too, are great—blackened steak, tawny onions, and brilliant red bell peppers. The coulis can also be used as a (fat-free) salad dressing. Feel free to substitute rib-eyes, T-bones, small tenderloins, or your favorite cut for the New York steaks.

PEPPER COULIS

3 red bell peppers, roasted, peeled, and seeded (page 190)

1 Anaheim pepper, roasted, peeled, stemmed, and seeded (page 190)

2 jalapeño peppers, roasted, peeled, stemmed, and seeded (page 190)

3 cloves garlic, chopped

2 tablespoons balsamic vinegar

1/4 cup extra virgin olive oil

1 teaspoon ground cumin

1 teaspoon chopped cilantro

Salt

Freshly ground black pepper

3 tablespoons olive oil

5 large onions, julienned

4 (8-ounce) New York steaks

Salt

Freshly ground black pepper

To prepare the coulis, place the bell peppers, Anaheims, jalapeños, garlic, vinegar, olive oil, ground cumin, and cilantro in the bowl of a food processor and process until smooth. Season to taste with salt and pepper and set aside.

To prepare the onions, heat 2 tablespoons of the olive oil in a large sauté pan over high heat until smoking hot. Add the onions and do not stir until they start to brown, 2 to 5 minutes. Toss and allow onions to brown completely, about 3 minutes. Cook over medium heat, stirring occasionally, until the onions are tender and caramelized, 3 to 5 minutes. Keep the onions warm while you cook the steaks.

To prepare the steaks, preheat the oven to 350°. Heat the remaining tablespoon of oil in a large ovenproof sauté pan over high heat until smoking hot. Add the steaks and sear well for about 2 minutes on each side. Put the pan in the oven and cook for 5 to 8 minutes for rare to medium-rare doneness.

To serve, distribute the caramelized onions among 4 individual plates and place a steak on top of each one. Spoon the coulis over the steaks and serve hot.

Roasted Chicken with Lemon & Saffron

SERVES 2

I developed this recipe after having dinner at a friend's house, where the chicken served had been roasted stuffed with garlic, lemon, and rosemary. It sounds great, but the stuffing didn't infuse the meat with flavor. I stuffed the garlic, lemon, and rosemary under the skin and found it infused the meat beautifully with delicious flavors. I like to serve the chicken with basmati rice or couscous. You can even serve this with a yogurt sauce made with garlic and a dash of fresh lemon juice.

1 tablespoon peeled, chopped
    fresh ginger

3 cloves garlic, chopped

1/2 teaspoon saffron threads

1 teaspoon chopped cilantro

2 teaspoons chopped fresh basil

1 1/2 tablespoons olive oil

Juice of 1/2 lemon

1 (3- to 4-pound) whole roasting
chicken

1/2 lemon, sliced crosswise

Kosher salt

Cracked black pepper

2 to 3 carrots, peeled and coarsely
    chopped

1 white onion, coarsely chopped

1 green bell pepper,
    coarsely chopped

Preheat the oven to 425°. Place the ginger, garlic, saffron, cilantro, and basil in a small food processor or spice grinder and purée. Transfer the mixture to a small bowl, add the olive oil and lemon juice and mix well. Starting at the neck end, gently loosen the chicken skin from the meat. Lift the loosened skin and spread the mixture on the meat. Place the lemon slices on top of the herb spread and pat the skin back in place. Truss together the chicken legs with kitchen twine. Place the vegetables in the roasting pan. Season the chicken all over with the kosher salt and black pepper and place on the vegetables in the roasting pan.

Roast the chicken in the oven for about 15 minutes. Reduce the temperature to 350° and continue roasting until the chicken is cooked through and reaches an internal temperature of 155° (use an instant-read meat thermometer to test) and the juices run clear when the thigh is pierced with a fork, 45 to 50 minutes. Remove the chicken from the oven and let it cool for about 3 minutes before slicing. Slice the chicken and serve hot.

Grilled Tuna with Tomato, Olive & Herb Compote

SERVES 4

Because seafood is so perishable, it is important to buy it from a reliable vendor. If you buy seafood and discover it is not fresh, return it. I don't buy prewrapped seafood, but if you do, ask the grocer to open the package for you so you can smell it to judge its freshness before you buy it. Fresh fish never smells fishy.

The best way to store seafood is in the refrigerator with ice on it but

This colorful compote is mounded on top of the grilled tuna like a relish, which makes the dish a beautiful as well as a satisfying, delicious meal. Use ripe tomatoes for the best results. Sometimes we smoke the tomatoes first, which gives the compote a richer flavor.

HERB COMPOTE
2 teaspoons olive oil
3 cloves garlic, chopped
1 small sweet onion, minced
4 cups halved cherry tomatoes
1/2 cup kalamata olives, pitted and chopped
1/2 cup red wine
2 oil- or salt-packed anchovy fillets, finely chopped
1 teaspoon chopped fresh rosemary
2 teaspoons chopped fresh thyme
2 teaspoons extra virgin olive oil
Salt
Freshly ground black pepper

1 tablespoon olive oil
4 (6-ounce) tuna fillets
Salt
Freshly ground black pepper
2 tablespoons herbes de Provence
1 bunch fresh thyme

To prepare the compote, heat the olive oil over high heat until very hot. Add the garlic and onion and sauté until fragrant, about 2 minutes. Add the cherry tomatoes and olives and toss well with the onion mixture. Add the wine and reduce to about $^1/_4$ cup over over high heat, 3 to 4 minutes. Add the anchovies, rosemary, and thyme and cook for about 5 minutes. Add the olive oil and season to taste with salt and pepper. Keep warm until ready to serve.

To prepare the tuna, heat the olive oil in a large sauté pan over high heat until smoking hot. Season the tuna with the salt and pepper and the herbes de Provence. Place the tuna in the pan and sear each side for about 2 minutes. The fish will be very rare. (The longer fish is cooked, the drier it becomes.)

To serve, place the tuna on individual plates and top with a generous spoonful of the compote. Garnish with the fresh herbs and serve immediately.

not touching it, with a place for the water from the melting ice to collect. (For example, wrap the seafood in plastic, place it in a colander set over a bowl, and cover with ice.) It is best to store seafood at 40° for no longer than 2 days. If you will not be using it within that time period, freeze it, and thaw it before cooking.

Pepper-Rubbed Pork Chops with Warm Bacon & Cabbage Salad

SERVES 6

We sell a lot of pork at the restaurant—it outsells everything. Choose nice, thick chops. You don't want those little ones that curve up like a bowl as they cook. My mother used to get those—we found they were just perfect for the "pork jerky" she inadvertently made. Pork chops are particularly delicious with this unusual salad, which is one of my favorites. My German grandfather made great sauerkraut and pickles, and this salad recalls the tastes of my childhood. When I get a craving for it, I make a big bowl and eat it all by myself. The vinegar adds tanginess to the cabbage and cuts through the rich bacon. For even more texture, add sliced Granny Smith apples just before you serve it, and enjoy the crunchy apple, refreshing cabbage, and the crispy bacon.

BACON AND CABBAGE SALAD

8 slices bacon, diced

3 cloves garlic, chopped

1 onion, diced

3/4 cup dry sherry

1 small head cabbage, julienned

2 tablespoons sherry vinegar

1 tablespoon olive oil

2 teaspoons chopped fresh thyme

1/2 cup chopped walnuts, toasted (page 191)

Salt

Black pepper

2 tablespoons cracked black pepper

Salt

1/2 cup all-purpose flour

6 (8-ounce) pork chops

2 tablespoons olive oil

To prepare the salad, place the bacon in a medium sauté pan and cook over medium heat until crispy, about 3 minutes. Transfer the bacon to a paper towel to drain. Add the garlic and onion to the pan and sauté in the bacon grease over medium-high heat for about 2 minutes. Add the sherry and cook until reduced by half, 3 to 4 minutes. Add the cabbage and cook until tender, about 4 minutes. Add the sherry vinegar, olive oil, thyme, and walnuts and season to taste with salt and pepper. Keep warm until ready to use.

To prepare the pork chops, preheat the oven to 350°. Rub the meat with the black pepper and season with the salt. Put the flour on a plate and dredge the chops in the flour. Pat the chops gently to remove any excess flour.

Heat the olive oil in a very large, ovenproof sauté pan over high heat until smoking hot. Add the pork chops and sear for 2 minutes on each side. Place in the oven and cook for about 8 minutes, or until the meat reaches an internal temperature of 150° (use an instant-read meat thermometer to test). Remove from the oven.

To serve, place 1 pork chop on each plate. Spoon some of the cabbage salad alongside the chops and serve immediately.

Beef Tenderloins with Blue Cheese & Rosemary Vinaigrette

SERVES 4

MEATS

I like buying meat at a market with a genuine butcher counter so I can talk with the experts and pick up some tips while I shop. I always buy from a trustworthy butcher and try to stick to local meats. When selecting meat, choose pieces that are pink—the pinker the better. Any brown discoloration is usually just the result of oxidization, which is harmless, but you can be sure that the pinkest pieces are the freshest in the case. I prefer to buy fresh meat instead of frozen because, no matter how well you wrap it, freezing dries it out.

This Bistro dish is perfect for those times when you want to pull out all the stops. I love the tangy vinaigrette against the richness of the blue cheese. The vinaigrette keeps for weeks in the refrigerator and can be used on salads, in mashed potatoes, or even drizzled over roasted fingerling potatoes.

4 (6-ounce) beef tenderloins
6 ounces blue cheese
2 tablespoons milk
4 slices pepper bacon
1 tablespoon olive oil
Salt
Cracked black pepper

ROSEMARY VINAIGRETTE
1 shallot, chopped
2 cloves garlic, chopped
1 tablespoon Dijon mustard
1 tablespoon chopped fresh rosemary
1/2 teaspoon dry mustard powder
2 tablespoons wine vinegar
1/2 cup extra virgin olive oil
Salt
Cracked black pepper

Cut a ¹/2-inch horizontal slit in the side of the beef tenderloins. Place the cheese and milk in a small bowl and mix well with a fork. Put the mixture into a pastry bag without a tip in place (alternatively, you can put the mixture in a heavy freezer bag, work it down into one corner, and cut the end off). Using your fingers, open a pocket in one of the tenderloins. Pipe equal amounts of the cheese filling into the slits. Wrap the bacon slices around the sides of the tenderloin, tucking in the ends of the bacon to form a seal. Carefully place the tenderloins on a plate, cover with plastic wrap, and refrigerate.

To prepare the vinaigrette, place the shallot, garlic, mustard, rosemary, dry mustard, and vinegar in a medium bowl and whisk together. Slowly whisk in the olive oil until thickened and emulsified. Season to taste with salt and pepper and set aside.

To cook the tenderloins, preheat the oven to 350°. Heat the olive oil over high heat in a very large ovenproof sauté pan until smoking hot. Remove the tenderloins from the refrigerator, season them generously with salt and pepper, and place them in the pan. Sear tenderloins for about 2 minutes on each side. Put the pan in the oven and cook for 5 to 8 minutes for rare to medium-rare doneness. Remove from the oven and serve hot with vinaigrette.

Ling Cod with Ancho Chile Rub
& Tomatillo Salsa

SERVES 4

This coarsely chopped tomatillo salsa is John's recipe. It is essential that you use fresh tomatillos, which are available in Latin American markets and in the produce section of some supermarkets. You can also use small green tomatoes. The rich coffee-chocolate flavor from the ancho chiles makes all the difference in this dish. Ancho chiles are available in the dried chiles section of most supermarkets. We roast them, pulverize them, and use them all the time in soups and flour-dredging mixtures.

TOMATILLO SALSA
1 pound tomatillos, hulled and cored
4 whole cloves garlic
1 small red onion, coarsely chopped
2 fresh jalapeño peppers, halved and seeded
3 vine-ripened tomatoes, cored
1/2 cup olive oil
1/4 cup rice vinegar
1 teaspoon ground toasted cumin seeds (page 192)
1/2 teaspoon ground coriander
1 teaspoon chile powder
Pinch of salt

1/4 cup dried pulverized ancho chiles
1/2 cup all-purpose flour
4 (6-ounce) ling cod fillets
Salt

Oil and heat an electric grill to high, or light the barbecue coals.

To prepare the salsa, preheat the oven to 425°. Combine the tomatillos, garlic, onion, jalapeños, tomatoes, olive oil, and vinegar in a heavy roasting pan. Place in the oven and roast for about 45 minutes, or until the tomatillos start to brown and the tomatoes soften. Remove from the oven and let cool for about 10 minutes. Put the mixture into the bowl of a food processor and add the cumin, coriander, and chile powder. Pulse just until the mixture is coarsely chopped. Season with salt and set aside.

To prepare the fish, finely grind the ancho chiles in a coffee or spice grinder. Mix together the flour and ancho powder in a medium bowl and put the mixture on a plate. Season the fish with salt and dredge each piece in the flour mixture. Place the fish on the hot, well-oiled grill and grill for about 4 minutes on each side. Remove fish from the grill, place on individual plates, and serve immediately with the salsa spooned over the top.

Lamb Chops with Rosemary–Green Peppercorn Sauce

SERVES 4

MUSTARD

You should always have two basic mustards on hand: a good, strong French Dijon mustard, and a whole-grain mustard. These days, there are many delicious kinds on the market. I have six mustards in my home pantry. Some of my favorites are green peppercorn, roasted red bell pepper, and herb mustards. I also have Chinese hot mustard powder, which is mixed

Green peppercorns enliven this classic combination. I like brine-packed green peppercorns much more than dried ones, but keep in mind that the residue in the bottom of the container can be very hot. When I was training as a cook, this peppercorn sauce nearly took off a woman's head in the dining room. I felt bad, but the experience did not dim my enthusiasm for this powerful ingredient. I always serve lamb with potatoes, like the Seasoned Mashed Baked Potatoes on page 45.

PEPPERCORN SAUCE
1 cup red wine
2 shallots, chopped
2 cloves garlic, chopped
2 cups lamb or veal stock (page 186)
1/2 cup heavy whipping cream
1 teaspoon chopped fresh rosemary
1 teaspoon chopped green peppercorns
Salt
Freshly ground black pepper

8 (3- to 4-ounce) lamb chops
2 teaspoons olive oil
2 teaspoons chopped fresh rosemary
Salt
Freshly ground black pepper

To prepare the sauce, put the wine, shallots, and garlic in a heavy saucepan and reduce over high heat until about $^1/4$ cup of wine remains. Add the stock and reduce over high heat until about $^3/4$ cup of liquid remains. Add the cream and reduce again over high heat until just about 1 cup of liquid remains. Add the rosemary and peppercorns and season to taste with salt and pepper. Keep warm.

To prepare the lamb chops, heat the grill high. Drizzle the chops with the olive oil, rub with the rosemary, and season with salt and pepper. Place the chops on the hot grill and cook for about 3 to 4 minutes per side for medium-rare to medium doneness. Remove from the grill and serve hot with the green peppercorn sauce spooned over the top.

with warm water just before using. Before we got too busy, we used to make our own mustard at the Bistro. We still make it occasionally, just because it's so easy and good. (For the recipe, check out my last book, COOKING WITH CAPRIAL.)

Roasted Chicken Breasts with Fava Bean Ragout

SERVES 4

The Fava Bean Ragout makes this otherwise basic, homestyle recipe something special. Fava beans are meaty, creamy, and ultra-earthy and are finally getting the attention they deserve. If you haven't tried them, or don't eat them more than a couple of times a year, give this ragout a try—I guarantee you'll like what you've been missing.

FAVA BEAN RAGOUT

1 teaspoon olive oil
4 ounces pancetta, diced
1 onion, julienned
3 cloves garlic, chopped
2 cups fresh shelled and skinned fava beans (page 191)
1 cup chicken stock (page 184)
2 roasted red bell peppers, peeled, seeded, and diced (page 190)
1 tablespoon chopped fresh thyme
Salt
Freshly ground black pepper

1 teaspoon olive oil
4 chicken breasts, with bone
Salt
Cracked black pepper
2 teaspoons chopped fresh basil
1/2 teaspoon ground cayenne pepper

To prepare the ragout, heat the olive oil in a medium sauté pan over high. Add the pancetta to the pan and cook until crispy, about 4 minutes. Add the onion and lightly sauté for 2 to 3 minutes. Add the garlic and fava beans and toss with the onions. Add the stock, decrease the heat to medium-high, and simmer until tender, about 5 minutes. Add the bell peppers, thyme, and salt and pepper. Keep warm.

To prepare the chicken, preheat the oven to 350°. Heat the olive oil in a 10-inch ovenproof sauté pan, over high heat until smoking hot. Season the chicken breasts with the salt and pepper and place skin over side down in the hot oil. Sear well, 2 to 3 minutes. Remove the chicken from the heat and place in the oven. Bake in the oven for 10 to 15 minutes, or just until the breasts are cooked through. Remove from the oven.

To serve, ladle the warm ragout onto a large serving platter and place the roasted chicken breasts on top. Serve hot.

Spicy Asian-Style Seafood Stew

SERVES 6

At the Bistro, we make the stew base in advance and prepare the seafood to order. You also can make the base ahead and freeze it. That way, all you have to do is pull the base out of the freezer, buy fresh seafood, and put it together in 5 to 10 minutes.

1 tablespoon vegetable oil

1 tablespoon peeled, chopped fresh ginger

1 small onion, diced

3 cloves garlic, chopped

1 cup mirin wine

2 cups fish or seafood stock (pages 187, 188)

1 stalk lemongrass, cut on the diagonal into large pieces

1 pound mussels, scrubbed and debearded

1/2 pound clams, rinsed

1 pound (16 to 20) peeled shrimp

1/2 pound diced seasonal whitefish (such as rock cod, ling cod, or sturgeon)

1 tablespoon instant sour paste (optional)

2 teaspoons chopped fresh basil

1 teaspoon chopped cilantro

1 teaspoon chile paste

Soy sauce

Heat the oil in a 4-quart stockpot or saucepan over high heat until very hot. Add the ginger, onion, and garlic and sauté until fragrant. Add the mirin and cook over high heat until reduced by half. Add the fish stock and lemongrass and simmer for 10 to 15 minutes, then strain.

In a wok placed over high heat, add the mussels and clams and cook just until the shells start to open, 2 to 3 minutes. Pour the stock over the mussels and clams in the wok. Add the shrimp, whitefish, sour paste, basil, cilantro, and chile paste and cook just until the fish is cooked through, 3 to 5 minutes. Season to taste with soy sauce, ladle into bowls, and serve hot.

Braised Lamb Shanks
with Roasted Shallots & Dried Cherries

SERVES 6

We serve lamb shanks often in the fall and winter at the restaurant and also prepare them in our cooking classes. Lamb shanks tend to be very tough because they are from a part of the animal that gets a lot of exercise. Braising the meat with acidic substances like vinegar and wine breaks down that toughness and allows the best flavor to come through. Look for dried cherries at gourmet markets. I like to serve the shanks over couscous (use the recipe on page 66, minus the cumin and ginger).

- 2 tablespoons olive oil
- 8 shallots, peeled
- 6 whole cloves garlic
- 6 (10- to 12-ounce) lamb shanks
- Salt
- Freshly ground black pepper
- 1/2 cup all-purpose flour
- 1 cup red wine
- 2 1/2 cups lamb or veal stock (page 186)
- 3 tablespoons balsamic vinegar
- 1 cup dried cherries
- 1 tablespoon chopped fresh thyme

Preheat oven to 300°. Put the olive oil, shallots, and garlic in a large roasting pan, cover with a lid, and place in the oven. Roast for about 1 hour, or until the shallots and garlic are soft to the touch. Remove the pan from the oven and place on the stovetop over high heat. Season the shanks with salt and pepper. Place the flour on a large plate and dredge the lamb in it. Place the shanks in the pan and sear both sides well, about 2 minutes on each side. Add the wine and reduce over high heat by about half. Add the stock, vinegar, cherries, and thyme, cover with a lid, and place in the oven. Cook until tender, 1 to 1 1/2 hours. Remove the pan from the oven and season the broth to taste with the salt and pepper. Place the lamb on a serving platter. Slice and serve hot with the sauce spooned over.

Pork Roast with Pecan Stuffing & Creamy Mustard Sauce

SERVES 4

The flavor of this roast is enriched by the crunchy pecan stuffing and tangy, creamy mustard sauce. You can make the mustard sauce up to two weeks ahead, but you'll need to stuff the pork just before cooking it to prevent any bacteria from growing. (This is a rule to follow with all stuffed meats.) To ensure thorough and safe cooking, I also butterfly the pork and pound it with a large meat mallet so it will cook evenly.

Pecans are my favorite nut. I think they're essential for a delicious pork roast stuffing. The other essential is grain mustard (in addition to the Dijon mustard in the sauce). Grain mustard has whole mustard seeds in it and usually is described as "whole-grain" on the label. If you cannot find a whole-grain mustard, use a Dijon or any other good mustard with visible mustard seeds in it.

PECAN STUFFING	MUSTARD SAUCE
2 tablespoons olive oil	1/2 cup sherry wine
2 cloves garlic, chopped	1/2 cup brandy
1 small onion, diced	2 cloves garlic, chopped
1 cup ground toasted pecans (page 191)	2 shallots, chopped
1 cup diced French bread	1 1/2 cups heavy whipping cream
1/4 cup chicken stock (page 184)	1 teaspoon dry mustard powder
1/2 pound pork sausage	1 heaping tablespoon Dijon mustard
2 teaspoons chopped fresh thyme	1 heaping tablespoon whole-grain mustard
1/2 teaspoon dry mustard powder	2 teaspoon chopped fresh flat-leaf parsley
Salt	Salt
Freshly ground black pepper	Freshly ground black pepper
1 (3-pound) boneless pork roast	

To prepare the stuffing, heat 1 tablespoon of the olive oil in a medium sauté pan over high heat until very hot. Add the garlic and onion and lightly sauté for about 2 minutes. Let the mixture cool, then place it in a medium bowl. Add the pecans and diced bread, and mix well. Add the chicken stock and mix well. Add

continued

Pot Roast *continued*

the sausage, thyme, and mustard powder, and mix together. Season to taste with salt and pepper.

To butterfly the pork roast, beginning cutting about halfway down cut along the side of the roast until you are about $1/4$ inch from the other side (do not cut all the way through the meat). Open the roast like a book and place it on a sturdy work surface. Pound the meat well with a large meat mallet, evenly flattening the meat. Spread the filling evenly on the meat and roll the roast jelly-roll style. Wrap kitchen twine around the roll and tie securely.

Preheat the oven to $325°$. Heat the remaining 1 tablespoon of olive oil over high heat in a large ovenproof sauté pan until smoking hot. Place the stuffed pork in the pan and sear well on all sides, about 5 minutes. Place the pan in the oven and roast the pork slowly until the internal temperature reaches $155°$ (use an instant-read meat thermometer to test), about 40 minutes.

Meanwhile, prepare the sauce. Place the sherry, brandy, garlic, and shallots in a medium saucepan and reduce over high heat until about $1/4$ cup of liquid remains. Add the cream and cook until about 1 cup of liquid remains and the sauce is thick. Add the dry mustard, Dijon, and whole-grain mustard and mix well. Add the parsley, salt, and pepper and keep warm until ready to use.

Remove the roast from the oven and let it rest for about 3 minutes before slicing. Cut the twine and remove from the roast. Slice the pork $1/4$ inch thick and place the slices on a serving platter or on individual plates. Drizzle the sauce over the slices and serve hot.

Oven-Poached Halibut with Fennel & Orange

SERVES 4

In this dish, a flavorful stock is used to cook the fish. I use halibut, but you can substitute any seasonal whitefish. I also like to use ling cod or sturgeon.

POACHING LIQUID

2 teaspoons olive oil
1 small onion, julienned
3 cloves garlic, chopped
1 large bulb fennel, julienned
1/2 cup dry sherry
1/2 cup fish or vegetable stock
    (pages 187, 185)
Zest of 1 orange
Juice of 1 orange

4 (6-ounce) halibut fillets
Salt
Freshly ground black pepper
1 tablespoon unsalted butter
2 tablespoons chopped fresh fennel greens

Preheat the oven to 350°. To prepare the poaching liquid, heat the olive oil in a large ovenproof sauté pan over high heat until very hot. Add the onion and garlic and sauté until fragrant, 1 to 2 minutes. Add the fennel and sauté for about 2 minutes more, then add the sherry, stock, and orange zest and juice, and reduce by about half.

To prepare the fish, season the fillets with salt and pepper and place in the poaching liquid. Add the butter and 1 tablespoon of fennel greens and cover with a lid or with aluminum foil. Place the pan in the oven and cook for 8 to 10 minutes, or until just cooked through.

Remove from the oven and place the fillets in 4 large, shallow soup bowls. Season the poaching liquid with salt and pepper and pour over the fillets. Top with the remaining orange zest and fennel and serve.

Spaghettini with Seared Scallops & Arugula

SERVES 6

This is a delicious and easy summer pasta. Use good-quality Parmesan and extra virgin olive oil. I use sea scallops because they are so quick and easy to cook. If you use the smaller bay scallops instead, be very careful not to overcook them. You can use shrimp in place of scallops. I also use a little truffle oil or lemon olive oil sometimes. If possible, use just-picked fresh parsley.

1 pound dried spaghettini
1 tablespoon vegetable oil
1 1/2 pounds sea scallops, cleaned
Kosher salt
Freshly ground black pepper
1/2 cup extra virgin olive oil
1/2 pound arugula
3 cloves garlic, chopped
1/3 cup chopped fresh flat-leaf parsley
1/2 teaspoon cracked black pepper
1 cup freshly grated Parmesan cheese

In a 6-quart saucepan or stockpot, bring about 10 cups of salted water to a rolling boil. Add the spaghettini and cook for 7 to 8 minutes, or until al dente.

Meanwhile, heat the vegetable oil in a sauté pan over high heat until smoking hot. Season the scallops with salt and pepper, add them to the pan, and sear for 1 to 2 minutes per side, or until just barely cooked through. Place the seared scallops in a large bowl. Add the extra virgin olive oil, arugula, garlic, parsley, pepper, and about half of the Parmesan cheese and toss to combine.

Drain the pasta in a colander and add it to the scallop mixture. Quickly toss well and transfer to a serving platter or on individual plates. Top with the remaining cheese and serve hot.

OLIVE OIL

Olive oil is like wine. There are many producers of olive oil, and there are many flavors and types. Olive oils can be green or golden, fruity or spicy, heavy or light. I advise buying small bottles of olive oil and comparing the tastes of each before you invest in a supersize container of any one variety.

COLD-PRESSED EXTRA VIRGIN OLIVE OIL

This is a must for salads. You would not want to cook with this kind of oil because it is so expensive and it has a lower burning point than other oils, making it difficult to get the oil hot enough to cook with before it literally goes

Seafood Linguine with Lemon & Basil Sauce

SERVES 4

We often have a seafood pasta on the menu at the Bistro, and I thought I'd include it in this book because readers keep asking for one. I add the cooked linguine at the end. Feel free to use other types of pasta besides linguine, which is traditionally used because it's neither too thick nor thin to hold up to the sauce and seafood.

- 2 teaspoons olive oil
- 3 cloves garlic, chopped
- 1 small onion, julienned
- 1/2 pound fresh clams, rinsed
- 1/2 pound mussels, scrubbed and debearded
- 1/2 cup dry sherry
- 1/2 pound (16 to 20) peeled shrimp
- 1 pound seasonal whitefish (such as cod or halibut), diced
- 1 cup heavy whipping cream
- Zest of 1 lemon
- Juice of 1/2 lemon
- 3 tablespoons chopped fresh basil
- 1/2 cup freshly grated Parmesan cheese
- 1 pound fresh linguine, cooked al dente
- Salt
- Cracked black pepper

In a very large sauté pan, heat the olive oil over high heat until very hot. Add the garlic and onion and lightly sauté until fragrant, about 1 minute. Add the clams and mussels and cook just until they start to open, about 3 minutes. Add the sherry and reduce by half over high heat. Add the shrimp, whitefish, and cream and cook until the cream starts to thicken and the shrimp just turn pink, 2 to 3 minutes. Add the zest, lemon juice, 1 tablespoon of the basil, and half of the Parmesan cheese and bring to a boil. Add the cooked pasta and bring to a boil again. Season to taste with salt and pepper. Transfer to a serving platter. Sprinkle the remaining Parmesan cheese and the basil over the top. Garnish with lemon slices and serve hot.

up in smoke. I use extra virgin olive oil for marinades, dressings, and for finishing sauces or dishes. For cooking, I use a grade of pure olive oil; it holds up well over high heat.

INFUSED OILS

We make a lot of infused olive oils at the restaurant. These days, oils are infused with everything from sage to truffles and are available in supermarkets as well as gourmet food stores. Store infused oils in the refrigerator.

Braised Chuck Roast
with Balsamic Vinegar, Figs & Port

SERVES 6

VINEGAR

There many kinds of vinegars. You can choose from a whole range of wonderful flavored vinegars these days, but be careful—sometimes you can get too many flavors competing in a dish. Vinegars vary in acidity. Rice wine vinegar and balsamic vinegar have a lower acidity level than other types and are good in salad dressings. Good vinegar is vital to a good salad. If you are using balsamic vinegar, it should be at least five years old. When you dress a salad with balsamic vinegar you can sometimes get away with using very little or

One day I came home from the market and discovered the butcher had wrapped up the wrong cut. I had asked for a top round roast and had been given a chuck roast, and I was disappointed. But John and I decided to make lemonade out of our lemon. We thought of a dish our chef, Mark Dowers, made once for a holiday "dine around," a wonderful stew of lamb, figs, and oranges. With that in mind, I braised the meat in olive oil, basalmic vinegar, stock, lots of herbs, figs, and a little port to add even more depth, and to our surprise, we had a great dish! If you're like us, you may tend to overlook chuck roasts because of what our mothers did to them. How dry they were! This braising method opens up a whole world of possibilities.

It's a good idea to keep a quality Port wine on hand for recipes like this one. You can get a good bottle for under fifteen dollars. If you don't have Port, use the heaviest dry red wine you can find, a Zinfandel or Cabernet, something with a lot of body.

1 (4-pound) chuck roast
Salt
Freshly ground black pepper
1/2 cup all-purpose flour
1 tablespoon olive oil
1 small onion, diced
3 cloves garlic, chopped
1/2 pound dried Mission figs, halved lengthwise
1/2 cup red wine
1/2 cup Port
2 cups veal or chicken stock (pages 186, 184)
1 tablespoon chopped fresh thyme

Preheat the oven to 350°. Season the roast with salt and pepper. Put the flour on large plate and dredge the meat in the flour. Place the oil in a roasting pan and heat it in the oven or on a burner over high heat until the oil is smoking hot. Add the roast and brown each side well, 3 to 4 minutes. Add the onion and garlic and sauté until fragrant, about 1 minute. Add the figs, red wine, and Port and cook over high heat until reduced by half. Add the stock and bring to a boil. Add the thyme, cover the roasting pan with a lid, and place in the oven. Cook until tender, about 1 hour.

Remove the pan from the oven and place the roast on a cutting board, reserving the braising liquid in the pan for the sauce. Slice the roast against the grain, cutting 1/4-inch-thick pieces, and put the slices on a serving plate. Season the sauce in the pan to taste with salt and pepper. If the sauce is thin, place the pan on a burner over high heat and reduce until thick enough to coat the back of a spoon. Ladle sauce over the sliced meat and serve hot.

no oil because the acidity can be so low. I avoid using seasoned rice wine vinegar, except in Asian dishes that need a sweet touch. I like sherry vinegars, which are rich and nutty and Cabernet vinegars, which are also rich but have more berry flavors than the sherry vinegars. Try using a Cabernet vinegar when a recipe calls for red wine vinegar.

Greek-Style Lamb Salad with Feta-Lemon Dressing

SERVES 4

This is not your regular Greek salad. The ground lamb is flavored with onions and garlic, and the mixture of spinach and wild greens adds texture and different flavors. I also add lots of vegetables so all you need is a crusty loaf of bread and you're set.

FETA-LEMON DRESSING

2 tablespoons red wine vinegar

2 cloves garlic, chopped

2 shallots, chopped

2 teaspoons chopped fresh oregano

1 teaspoon chopped fresh thyme

Zest of 1 lemon

Juice of 1 lemon

3/4 cup extra virgin olive oil

1/2 cup good-quality feta cheese

Salt

Freshly ground black pepper

LAMB SALAD

2 teaspoons olive oil

3 cloves garlic, chopped

1/2 onion, diced

1 1/2 pounds ground lamb

1 bunch fresh spinach, cleaned

1/4 pound mesclun or wild greens mix

2 roasted red bell peppers, peeled,
   seeded, and diced (page 190)

1 red onion, julienned

1 cucumber, thinly sliced

1 ripe tomato, cut into wedges

1/2 cup pine nuts, toasted

To prepare the dressing, put the vinegar, garlic, shallots, oregano, thyme, zest, and juice in a medium bowl and mix well. Slowly whisk in the olive oil until the dressing is thickened and emulsified. Add the feta and stir to mix. Season to taste with salt and pepper and stir again. Set aside.

To prepare the salad, heat the olive oil in a medium sauté pan until very hot. Add the garlic and onion and lightly sauté for 2 to 3 minutes. Add the lamb and cook just until cooked through, 3 to 5 minutes. Remove the pan from the heat and let the lamb cool slightly. Drain and discard the fat.

Put the spinach and mixed greens in a large bowl and toss with the bell peppers, onion, and cucumber. Add the cooked lamb and about 2 tablespoons of dressing per person and toss well. Place the salad on individual plates and top with the tomato wedges and pine nuts. Serve immediately with additional dressing on the side.

Grilled Flank Steak
with Sauce Vera Cruz & Guacamole

SERVES 6

ONIONS

Onions, a lily relative, are highly valued by cooks. Imagine cooking without them! There are two kinds of onions: green onions, or scallions, and dry or cured onions, which have a papery, brown skin.

Onions vary in flavor. White onions are the most potent, yellow onions are next, then red onions, and sweet onions are the gentlest of all. Red onions or Italian onions are best raw because they do not hold up well when cooked. Some cooks use the various types interchangeably, but I like to use raw red onions only

Get out the Mexican pottery and whip up a batch of margaritas—this is a festive dish for a Mexican meal. The Sauce Vera Cruz is a spicy tomato-based sauce, and the guacamole is far from the common type, which I find bland. My guacamole uses lots of roasted ground cumin, fresh lime and lemon juices, fresh tomatoes, salt, and garlic. I like to mash the avocado with a potato masher so the guacamole is chunky. Flank steak is the most flavorful cut of meat, but it can be tough if you overcook it, so be sure to keep an eye on the time.

SAUCE VERA CRUZ

2 teaspoons olive oil
2 cloves garlic, chopped
1 small red onion, diced
2 poblano chiles, roasted, peeled, stemmed, and seeded (page 190)
3 ripe tomatoes, cored, seeded, and diced
1 cup tomato purée
1/3 cup pitted and diced cured green olives
2 teaspoons chopped fresh oregano
Salt
Freshly ground black pepper

GUACAMOLE

2 ripe Haas avocados
2 cloves garlic, minced
1 small tomato, seeded and chopped
1/2 small onion, minced
Juice of 1 lime
2 teaspoons ground toasted cumin seeds (page 192)
1 tablespoon Durkee's cayenne sauce
Salt
Freshly ground black pepper

2 teaspoons olive oil
1 (3- to 4-pound) flank steak
Salt
Freshly ground black pepper

Brush the grill racks with oil and heat the grill to very hot. Meanwhile, prepare the sauce and guacamole.

To prepare the sauce, heat the olive oil in a medium saucepan over high heat until very hot. Add the garlic and onion and sauté lightly for 2 to 3 minutes. Add the chiles, tomatoes, and tomato purée and cook over high heat for about 5 minutes. Add the olives and oregano and cook for about 5 minutes. With a handheld blender, coarsely purée the sauce in the pan. Alternatively, transfer the sauce to the bowl of a food processer and blend, then return to the pan. Season to taste with salt and pepper and keep warm.

To prepare the guacamole, cut the avocados in half, remove the pits, and scoop the flesh out of the skins into a medium bowl. Add the garlic, tomato, onion, and lime juice and mash with a potato masher. Stir in the cumin, and cayenne sauce. Season to taste with the salt and pepper. Cover the bowl with plastic wrap and place in the refrigerator until ready to use.

To prepare the steak, rub the meat with olive oil and season it on both sides with salt and pepper. Place the meat on the very hot grill and cook for 2 to 3 minutes per side for rare to medium-rare doneness. Remove meat from the grill, place on a cutting board, and slice thinly against the grain at a 45-degree angle. Place the slices on a serving platter or on individual plates and spoon warm sauce generously over the slices. Top with a dollop of guacamole and serve hot.

for finishing dishes or to lightly cook them.

To chop onions without tears, put them in the refrigerator or freezer for fifteen minutes before cutting and always use a sharp knife.

When buying onions, choose those that are tight and have good color. Squeeze them to be sure they are firm and examine them closely, looking for any mildew or mold that might be under the skin. Store onions in a cool, dry place.

Five-Spice Roasted Duck
with Shiitake Mushroom Aioli

SERVES 4

Many people think of roasted duck as restaurant food, but it's actually easy to do at home. The duck and mushroom aioli are rich—a perfect treat for a family supper on a lazy Sunday.

2 (3-pound) ducks
2 to 4 cups water
2 tablespoons five-spice powder
Kosher salt
Szechwan peppercorns
3 cups water

SHIITAKE MUSHROOM AIOLI
1 cup white wine
2 1/2 cups sliced shiitake mushrooms
1 tablespoon peeled, chopped fresh ginger
3 cloves garlic
1/4 cup rice vinegar
1 egg yolk
1 1/2 cups vegetable oil
1 teaspoon minced cilantro
1 teaspoon chile paste
Soy sauce

To prepare the ducks, preheat the oven to 375°. Put the ducks on a rack in a roasting pan. Add the water, making sure the rack is above the water and no water touches the ducks. Place the pan in the oven and steam for 20 to 30 minutes. Remove the pan from the oven and discard the liquid. Season the ducks with the five-spice powder, salt, and pepper. Place the pan in the oven and roast until the duck reaches an internal temperature of 155° (use an instant-read meat thermometer to test) and is golden brown, 20 to 30 minutes.

Meanwhile, prepare the aioli. Place the wine and shiitake mushrooms in a medium sauté pan and cook over high heat until dry, 5 to 6 minutes. Put the mushrooms in the bowl of a food processor, add the ginger, garlic, vinegar, and yolk and process until smooth. With the machine running, slowly add the oil, cilantro, and chile paste through the feeder tube and process to purée well. Season to taste with the soy sauce.

Remove the duck from the oven. Cut off the legs and slice the breast. Place the meat on a serving platter and serve with the aioli in a bowl on the side.

Note: Individuals who are immunosuppressed and children should not eat uncooked eggs that have not been pasteurized.

Vegetarian Entrées

Crispy Potato Pancakes with Mediterranean Relish

SERVES 4

This recipe was inspired by John's Swiss Potatoes, which are one of my favorite potato dishes. These pancakes are satisfyingly crispy and tender. If you make the relish in advance, be sure you don't overcook it when you warm it up. You can also serve this relish with fish, grilled portobello mushrooms, or even poached eggs. Or, toss it with spaghettini and a little Parmesan or goat cheese.

4 Yukon gold potatoes
1 tablespoon olive oil
2 tablespoons unsalted butter
Salt
Freshly ground black pepper
Mediterranean Vegetable Relish (page 189)
1/2 cup crumbled feta cheese
1/3 cup plain yogurt or sour cream (optional)

To prepare the pancakes, bring a stockpot of water to a brisk boil. Drop in the potatoes and boil just until they are slightly softened yet still firm, about 10 minutes. Drain and set aside to cool. When cool enough to handle, grate the potatoes. Heat the olive oil on high heat in a 12-inch nonstick sauté pan until very hot. Add all of the grated potatoes and press to compact them into one large pancake. Cook the potato pancake for about 8 minutes, or until golden brown. Rub about 1 tablespoon of the butter around the side of the pan. Turn the pancake with a large spatula and brown the other side well, about 8 minutes. Just before the pancake is finished, rub the remaining 1 tablespoon of butter around the edge of the pan. Season the pancake well with salt and black pepper and slide it onto a large serving platter. Mound the relish in the center of the pancake, top with the feta, and a dollop of yogurt or sour cream. Cut into wedges and serve immediately.

Double-Crust Mushroom Pie

SERVES 6

I like a dollop of sour cream or crème fraîche with this down-home, yet elegant, pie. With a green salad and a glass of merlot, it's a great fall meal.

FILLING
1 tablespoon olive oil
1 onion, julienned
3 cloves garlic, chopped
4 cups sliced wild mushrooms (such as chanterelles, morels, or oyster mushrooms)
4 cups sliced button mushrooms
1 cup red wine
1/4 cup balsamic vinegar
2 teaspoons chopped fresh rosemary
2 teaspoons chopped fresh thyme
Salt
Freshly ground black pepper

Savory Pie Crust (page 190)
1/2 cup grated good-quality Swiss cheese

To prepare the filling, heat the olive oil in a very large sauté pan over high heat until very hot. Add the onion and garlic and sauté until fragrant, about 2 minutes. Add the mushrooms and sauté until just tender, 5 to 6 minutes. Add the red wine and reduce heat until about $1/2$ cup of liquid remains. Add the vinegar, rosemary, and thyme and reduce again until about $1/2$ cup of liquid remains. Season to taste with salt and pepper and let cool completely.

Preheat the oven to 425°. Cut the dough in half. On a very well-floured board, roll the dough out to a 10-inch circle. Place the rolled-out crust in the bottom of a 9-inch pie pan. Sprinkle the crust evenly with the Swiss cheese and pour the filling over it. Roll out the second half of the dough. Cover the filling with the second crust and crimp the edges to seal the crusts together. Place the pie on the center rack of the oven and bake for about 15 minutes. Decrease the heat to 350° and bake for 25 to 30 minutes more, or until golden brown. Remove the pie from the oven and let rest for about 5 minutes before slicing.

To serve, slice the pie into wedges and serve on individual plates.

Roasted Vegetable–Goat Cheese Flan

SERVES 4

This is a delicious custard of roasted vegetables and eggs. My friend Diana served a caramelized onion flan at the Rain City Grill in Seattle, a restaurant she owned with her husband, Tom. I loved the creamy, rich flavor and wanted to capture a little of that in this recipe. The goat cheese lightens it up and makes it tangy.

1 tablespoon olive oil
5 whole cloves garlic
4 shallots, peeled and halved lengthwise
1 small onion, diced
1 small celeriac, peeled and diced
2 carrots, peeled and diced
1 large sweet potato, peeled and diced
1 cup asparagus sliced on the diagonal
2 tablespoons balsamic vinegar
2 cups heavy whipping cream
1/2 cup soft fresh goat cheese
5 eggs, slightly beaten
1/2 teaspoon salt
1/2 teaspoon freshly ground black pepper

CHEESE

I use the following four cheeses more than any others:

GOAT CHEESE (CHÉVRE)

A soft, tangy cheese. Many good local goat cheeses are available today.

FETA

A tangy, salty cheese made with sheep's, cow's, or goat's milk. Some are milder, some tangier, some saltier than others, but I prefer sheep's milk feta.

PARMESAN

Parmesan adds zing to many foods, including green salads and pizza. It is also good for browning casseroles and finishing pastas. Buy the best quality Parmesan you can find, and grate it just before

Preheat the oven to 425°. In a large ovenproof sauté pan, heat the olive oil over high heat until very hot. Add the garlic, all of the vegetables except the asparagus and place the pan in the oven. Roast for 35 to 40 minutes, or until the vegetables start to brown and are almost tender. Add the asparagus and vinegar and cook for 5 minutes more. When the vegetables are tender, remove the pan from the oven and set aside to let them cool completely.

Reduce the oven temperature to 350°. Butter a 2-quart soufflé dish. Place the cooled vegetables in a large bowl. Add the cream and goat cheese, and stir to mix thoroughly. Add the eggs, stir well, and season with the salt and pepper. Pour the mixture into the soufflé dish. Bake on the center rack of the oven for 40 to 50 minutes, or until a knife inserted in the center comes out clean. Remove from the oven. Spoon portions onto individual plates and serve warm.

using. The powdered Parmesan in a can is not even worth eating. The difference in flavor between the powdered and freshly grated cheese is like the difference between sawdust and whipped cream. Parmesan is a great cheese to use if you want to reduce your fat intake because it is made with skim milk.

RICOTTA

This soft Italian cheese is most often used in pasta dishes and fillings. I recommend using a whole-milk ricotta because it has a fuller taste than the lower fat types. I recently had some great ricotta—it was so fresh and creamy that it made me realize there's a greater scope of possibilities for this soft Italian cheese than we might think.

Marinated Grilled Portobello Mushrooms with Spicy Pepper Sauce

SERVES 6

Portobello mushrooms are wonderful because they are so meaty and dense that they absorb flavors well and hold up well when grilled—they don't just turn to mush. Don't marinate the mushrooms for more than six hours or the flavors will become too strong. I like to serve the grilled caps on a bed of mashed potatoes, but you can substitute soft polenta (page 132) if you prefer.

MARINADE

4 cloves garlic, chopped
2 teaspoons chopped fresh thyme
1 teaspoon chopped fresh rosemary
1 teaspoon cracked black pepper
1/4 cup red wine vinegar
2/3 cup extra virgin olive oil

6 extra large portobello mushrooms (6 to 8 inches in diameter)

SPICY PEPPER SAUCE

1 cup red wine
3 cloves garlic, chopped
2 shallots, chopped
2 cups roasted vegetable stock (page 185)
1 jalapeño pepper, roasted, peeled, stemmed, and seeded (page 190)
2 Anaheim peppers, roasted, peeled, stemmed and seeded (page 190)
1 teaspoon ground coriander
2 teaspoons ground toasted cumin seeds (page 192)
1 teaspoon chopped cilantro
2 teaspoons unsalted butter
Salt
Freshly ground black pepper
Seasoned Mashed Baked Potatoes (page 45)

CUMIN

Cumin is a rich, earthy spice, essential in many Middle Eastern, Asian, and Mediterranean dishes. It is most commonly used in curries and chile powders, but it is also delicious in hummus, black bean soup, and other dishes. It should be purchased in small quantities and stored in an airtight container in a cool, dark place for no more than six months.

The cumin seed is similar in shape to a caraway seed, something like a tiny crescent moon. The aromatic, nutty seed is available

To prepare the marinade, put all of the ingredients in a small bowl and whisk together. Remove the stems from the portobellos and discard them. Place the mushroom caps in a large bowl, pour the marinade over them, and toss well. Let marinate for at least 30 minutes.

To prepare the sauce, put the red wine, garlic, and shallots in a medium saucepan and reduce over high heat until about $1/3$ cup of liquid remains, about 4 minutes. Add the vegetable stock and peppers, decrease the heat to medium, and reduce until about half of the liquid remains. Purée the sauce in the pan with a handheld blender. Alternatively, transfer the sauce to the bowl of a food processor and blend, then return to the pan. Season to taste with the coriander, cumin, and cilantro. Add the butter, and stir well. Season to taste with the salt and pepper. Keep warm.

To prepare the mushrooms, oil the grill racks and heat the grill to very hot. Remove the mushrooms from the marinade, letting the excess marinade drain off, and place the caps on the grill. Grill on each side for 3 to 4 minutes, or until tender.

To serve, divide the mashed potatoes or polenta among the serving plates. Spoon the mushrooms over them and pour some of the sauce over the top. Serve immediately with the remaining sauce in a bowl on the side.

in three colors: white, black, and amber (all sold in gourmet and Asian markets). White and amber are similar in taste; the black seed has a more peppery flavor.

Powdered cumin is the ground seed. As with all seeds, grinding it just before using maximizes its flavor. You can grind the seeds in an electric spice mill or by hand with a mortar and pestle. Always toast ground cumin before using to heighten flavor and eliminate potential grittiness. (For toasting instructions, see page 192.)

Pasta with Caramelized Onion Sauce and Spicy Pepper Tapenade

SERVES 4

This dish has interesting flavor and color contrasts. The rich onion sauce contrasts with the tangy tapenade and the caramel-colored pasta contrasts with the bright red and green of the tapenade. The caramelized onion sauce takes a while to make, but you can make it up to a week ahead. I recommend penne pasta because the sauce gets trapped inside the tubes for a delicious surprise.

ONION SAUCE

2 tablespoons olive oil

4 onions, julienned

1/2 cup dry sherry

1/2 cup dry red wine

2 cloves garlic, chopped

1 cup roasted vegetable stock (page 185)

1 tablespoon chopped fresh thyme

Salt

Freshly ground black pepper

TAPENADE

1 red bell pepper, roasted, peeled, and seeded (page 190)

2 Anaheim chiles, roasted, peeled, stemmed, and seeded (page 190)

3 cloves garlic

1 teaspoon capers

2 salt- or oil-packed anchovy fillets

1 tablespoon rice vinegar

1/4 cup extra virgin olive oil

Pinch of salt

3/4 pound dried penne

3/4 cup finely grated Gouda cheese

To prepare the onion sauce, heat the olive oil in a very large sauté pan over high heat until smoking hot. Add the onions and cook without stirring, for at least 2 minutes to caramelize. Toss the onions and let sit, without stirring for 2 to 3 minutes. Toss again and continue to cook until the onions are browned and well caramelized, 6 to 8 minutes more. Add the sherry, red wine, and garlic and deglaze, scraping the bottom of the pan to gather all of the browned bits. Let the wine reduce by about half and add the garlic and vegetable stock. Reduce again by about half. Add the thyme and season to taste with salt and pepper. Set aside.

To prepare the tapenade, put the bell pepper, Anaheim chile, garlic, capers, anchovies, and vinegar in the bowl of a food processor fitted with the metal blade. Run the machine for about 30 seconds to coarsely chop. Add the olive oil and process again to mix. Transfer the tapenade to a medium bowl, season with the salt, and set aside.

To prepare the pasta, bring 2 quarts of salted water to a rolling boil in a large saucepan. Add the pasta and cook until al dente, about 8 to 10 minutes. Drain the pasta in a colander. Return the sauce to the heat and bring to a boil. Add the pasta and toss well.

To serve, place the pasta on a serving platter or on individual pasta plates. Top with the tapenade and grated Gouda cheese. Serve immediately.

Roasted Vegetable Paella

SERVES 4

Paella is a traditional rice dish from Spain, where cooks add everything from squid to rabbit to their family-sized paella pans. This oven-roasted vegetarian version is enriched with a whole head of garlic that's roasted right along with the vegetables as the rice cooks. It's easy and elegant.

2 tablespoons olive oil

1 whole head garlic

3 cloves garlic, chopped

1 onion, diced

4 potatoes, peeled and cut into 1/4-inch-thick slices

4 large ripe tomatoes, peeled, seeded, and diced

6 cups vegetable stock (page 185)

3 cups uncooked long-grain white rice

1 teaspoon saffron threads

2 bay leaves

1 teaspoon good-quality paprika

Salt

Freshly ground black pepper

Preheat the oven to 350°. Heat the olive oil in a Dutch oven or large paella pan. With a sharp knife, cut the top off the head of garlic, exposing just the tips of the tops of the cloves. Add the head of garlic and sauté lightly for 2 to 3 minutes. Add the chopped garlic, onion, and potatoes and sauté well, about 4 minutes. Add the tomatoes and stock and bring to a boil. Add the rice, saffron, bay leaves, paprika, and salt and pepper. Cover with a lid and bake in the oven until the rice is tender, about 20 minutes. Remove the pan from the oven. Remove the head of garlic from the paella and squeeze the roasted garlic from the cloves into the paella. Stir to mix.

To serve, spoon the paella onto a large platter or individual plates and serve hot.

Vegetable Stew with Rich Red Wine Sauce

SERVES 4

This is a vegetable stew with a hearty, rich sauce made by reducing the vegetable stock to almost a demi-glace before adding the wine. The vegetables need to be perfectly cooked in an all-vegetable stew. If you make this a day ahead, remove it from the heat while the vegetables are still undercooked and finish cooking the stew right before you plan to serve it. The stew is great on its own, or ladled over mashed potatoes (page 45) or soft polenta (page 132).

2 tablespoons olive oil

6 shallots, halved lengthwise

3 cloves garlic, chopped

1 onion, diced

5 carrots, peeled and cut into large dice

1 turnip, peeled and cut into large dice

3 large potatoes, peeled and cut into large dice

1 large sweet potato, peeled and cut into large dice

3 red bell peppers, roasted, peeled, seeded, and diced (page 190)

1/2 cup all-purpose flour

2 cups red wine

3 cups roasted vegetable stock (page 185)

1 tablespoon chopped fresh rosemary

2 teaspoons chopped fresh thyme

1 teaspoon chopped fresh marjoram

2 tablespoons Durkee's cayenne sauce

Salt

Freshly ground black pepper

Heat the olive oil in a large stockpot over high heat until very hot. Add the shallots and cook until they start to caramelize. Add the garlic, toss, and cook lightly for 1 to 2 minutes. Meanwhile, put all of the diced vegetables in a bowl and toss with the flour. Add the vegetables to the stockpot and brown for 4 to 5 minutes. Add the red wine and reduce until about 1/2 cup of liquid remains. Add the stock and fresh herbs and cook, covered, until the vegetables are tender. Stir in the cayenne sauce. Season to taste with salt and pepper.

To serve, place the stew in a large serving bowl and serve hot.

Asian Vegetable Stir-Fry with Basmati Rice

SERVES 4

BASMATI RICE

2 teaspoons vegetable oil
1 tablespoon peeled, chopped fresh ginger
1 1/2 cups basmati rice
3 cloves garlic, chopped
3 cups vegetable stock (page 185)
1/4 cup heavy cream
Pinch of salt
Pinch of freshly ground black pepper

STIR FRY

2 teaspoons vegetable oil
3 cloves garlic, chopped
1 tablespoon peeled, chopped fresh ginger
1 onion, julienned
3 carrots, peeled and cut thinly on the diagonal
2 zucchini, cut thinly on the diagonal
3 red bell peppers, seeded and julienned
1 cup fresh bean sprouts
1 cup fresh peas
1 cup vegetable stock (page 185)
2 teaspoons curry paste or curry powder
3 tablespoons sweet, hot chile sauce
    plus additional, as needed
1 teaspoon cornstarch
Soy sauce plus additional, as needed

CHILES

Chiles come in many forms:

FRESH CHILES

Anaheims, poblanos, and jalapeños should all find their way into your cooking. Generally, the smaller the pepper the hotter. All are hotter when you include the pith inside the chile. When I cook with fresh peppers, I add less than the recipe calls for and then adjust for spiciness to taste.

DRIED CHILES

We use roasted anchos in soups, sauces, and dressings, and to season dredging flour. Wear protective gloves when crushing or breaking dried hot chiles.

CHILE PASTE

A Chinese condiment made from fermented

To prepare the rice, preheat the oven to 350°. Heat the oil in an ovenproof saucepan over high heat until hot. Add the ginger and lightly sauté for about 1 minute. Rinse the basmati under running water and add it to the pan. Add the garlic and toss to mix, then add the stock and cream. Stir well and bring to a boil. Add the salt and pepper, cover, place in the oven, and cook for about 15 minutes. Remove from the oven, stir well, and return to the oven for another 15 minutes. Meanwhile, prepare the stir-fry.

To stir-fry the vegetables, heat the oil in a wok or large sauté pan over high heat until very hot. Add the garlic, ginger, and onion and sauté for 2 to 3 minutes. Add the carrots and sauté for about 3 minutes, or until the carrots are crisp-tender. Add the zucchini and bell peppers and sauté for about 2 minutes. Add the bean sprouts, fresh peas, and stock and cook until the vegetables are just done and the stock is boiling, 2 to 3 minutes. Add the curry paste and chile sauce and toss well. Put the cornstarch in a bowl and stir in just enough water to soften it. Add the cornstarch to the pan and stir it into the sauce. Season to taste with the soy sauce and additional chile sauce, if desired.

To serve, place the rice on a serving platter or on individual plates and top with the stir-fry. Serve with extra soy sauce and chile sauce on the side.

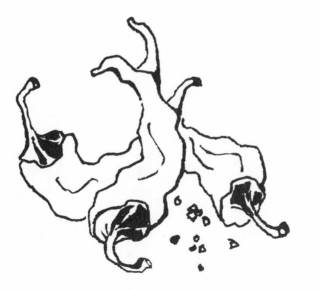

soybeans, red chiles, and, sometimes, garlic. I like Sambal Oelek, a Thai chile paste made from cooked chiles.

SWEET HOT CHILE SAUCE

This sauce goes by several different names and is used in Thai, Vietnamese, and Chinese cooking. I prefer chile sauce over dried chile flakes—it has a more interesting flavor and blends with other ingredients quicker. Sweet hot chile sauce is made from tomatoes, chiles, vinegar, water, salt, and sugar. You can use chile paste in place of chile sauce when you want less liquid. The paste is similar, but contains soybeans and has more substance to it. It keeps in a clean, airtight bottle in the refrigerator keep for up to a year.

Spaghetti Squash with Sundried Tomato–Rosemary Sauce

SERVES 4

Spaghetti squash is flavorful and nutritious and can be used in any dish in place of spaghetti. You can roast the spaghetti squash up to one week ahead so all you have to do is reheat it with the sauce to serve. The squash is a good vehicle for the flavors in the sauce, which we use regularly at the Bistro. Goat cheese or blue cheese are flavorful additions.

2 spaghetti squashes

SUNDRIED TOMATO–ROSEMARY SAUCE

3 cloves garlic, chopped

3 shallots, chopped

1/2 cup diced dry-packed sundried tomatoes

1 cup red wine

2 cups heavy whipping cream

2 teaspoons chopped fresh rosemary

Salt

Freshly ground black pepper

4 ounces thinly shaved Parmesan cheese

4 sprigs rosemary

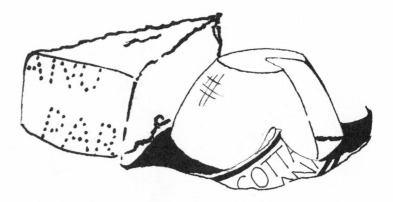

To prepare the squash, preheat the oven to 425°. Pierce the squash in several places with a fork. Put the squash in a roasting pan and roast in the oven until tender, 40 to 50 minutes.

Meanwhile, prepare the sauce. Place the garlic, shallots, sundried tomatoes, and wine in a saucepan and reduce over high heat until about $^1/_3$ cup of liquid remains. Add the cream and reduce until about 1 $^1/_2$ cups of liquid remains, about 10 minutes. Add the rosemary and cook over high heat for about 5 minutes more. Season to taste with salt and pepper and set aside.

Remove the squash from the oven and set aside until cool enough to handle. When cool, cut the squash in half lengthwise and, using a large spoon, remove and discard the seeds and any pith. Scrape the stringy squash flesh into a bowl and discard the skin. Season the squash with the salt and pepper and toss.

To serve, place the squash on a large serving platter and pour the reduced sauce over the top. Sprinkle the Parmesan shavings over the top, garnish with the rosemary sprigs, and serve hot.

Spicy Lentils Topped with Seared Onions, Sweet Peppers & Artichokes

SERVES 4

Nutritionists say that nonvegetarians should substitute legumes for meat at least once a week, which is just fine with me because I think they're delicious. I like the small dark green French lentils for their color and flavor and for the way they hold their shape. Here, the lentils are cooked and then tossed with a vinaigrette when they are hot. You can make the lentils ahead, if you like, and pour the warm vinaigrette over them when you are ready to eat.

2 teaspoons olive oil
1 small onion, diced
4 cloves garlic, diced
1 tablespoon peeled, chopped fresh ginger
2 fresh jalapeño peppers, diced
2 cups lentils
6 cups roasted vegetable stock (page 185)
1 teaspoon curry powder, toasted (page 192)
2 teaspoons ground cumin
Pinch of ground cinnamon
2 teaspoons Durkee's cayenne sauce
Salt
Freshly ground black pepper

1 tablespoon olive oil
2 onions, cut crosswise into 1/4-inch-thick slices
3 red bell peppers, cut into large dice
2 cups water-packed artichoke hearts
1 tablespoon chopped fresh basil
1/4 cup balsamic vinegar
Salt
Freshly ground black pepper

CURRY

Curry is an essential ingredient in Thai, Vietnamese, and Indian cooking, and it is also the name for dishes with a curry sauce. The word "curry" is from the southern Indian word "kari," which means sauce. Curries vary a great deal from region to region and cook to cook. My favorite curries are Vietnamese.

Curry powder, is a blend of up to 20 ground spices and herbs. In India, curry powder is ground fresh daily. The most common components are allspice, black pepper, cardamom, chiles, cayenne, cinnamon, cloves, coriander, cumin, fennel, fenugreek, ginger, mace, mustard, nutmeg, poppy and sesame seeds,

To prepare the lentils, heat the olive oil in a large saucepan over high heat until very hot. Add the onion, garlic, ginger, and jalapeño peppers and lightly sauté for about 2 minutes. Add the lentils, stock, curry, cumin, cinnamon, and cayenne sauce and cook until the lentils are tender. Season to taste with salt and pepper and keep warm.

Heat the oil in a very large sauté pan over high heat until smoking hot. Add the onions and sear well, 2 to 3 minutes. Toss and sear again for another 2 to 3 minutes. Add the bell peppers and toss and sear again for 2 to 3 minutes. Add the artichoke hearts, toss, and cook just to heat. Add the basil and vinegar and reduce until the liquid is almost evaporated. Season to taste with salt and pepper.

To serve, place the lentils on a large serving platter and top with the vegetables. Serve hot.

saffron, tamarind, and turmeric. Try mixing these spices to create your own personal blend. Curry powder should be stored in an airtight container in a cool, dark place for no more than two months. Curry powders should be toasted to maximize their flavor and remove any grittiness. (For toasting instructions, see page 192.) Thai-style curry paste is a concentrated blend of clarified butter, curry powder, vinegar, mace, poppy seed, and saffron. Thai cuisine features red, green, and yellow curries, made from corresponding blends of curry paste mixed with coconut milk. The paste stores well in the refrigerator.

Roasted Onions with Herbed Cheese Stuffing

SERVES 6

You can use any type of sweet yellow onion in season; I use our glorious Walla Wallas because they caramelize so nicely. The onions can be roasted a day ahead and refrigerated until you are ready to stuff them.

6 medium-large onions (just bigger than a baseball)

1/4 cup olive oil

STUFFING

1 tablespoon olive oil

3 cloves garlic

1/2 cup dry sherry

3 cups diced French bread

1 cup vegetable stock (page 185)

1/4 cup diced dry-packed sundried tomatoes

1/2 cup freshly grated Gouda cheese

1/2 cup freshly grated Parmesan cheese

2 teaspoons chopped fresh basil

1 teaspoon chopped fresh thyme

Salt

Freshly ground black pepper

Preheat the oven to 325°. Slice off the tops of the onions, cut part of the bottoms off (so they will sit flat), and peel them. Place the onions on a rack in a roasting pan and drizzle them with the olive oil. Place in the oven and bake until the onions are tender when pierced with a fork, about $1^1/2$ hours.

Remove the onions from the oven and let cool. Pull the centers out of the onions by pushing from the bottom with your fingers and gently pulling at the other end, leaving at least 3 layers intact inside. Set aside and reserve the centers of the onions.

To prepare the stuffing, dice the reserved centers of the onions. Heat the olive oil in a medium sauté pan over high heat until very hot. Add the diced onions and sauté until fragrant, about 2 minutes, then add the garlic and sauté for about 1 minute. Add the sherry and reduce by about half, then remove the pan from the heat and let cool.

Preheat the oven to 350°. Place the diced bread in a large bowl. Add the onion mixture and toss together. Add enough of the stock to moisten the bread and mix well. Add the tomatoes, Gouda, Parmesan, basil, and thyme and mix well. Season to taste with salt and pepper. Stuff each onion with a heaping $^1/2$ cup of filling. Place the stuffed onions on the rack in the roasting pan and bake until heated through, about 20 minutes. Remove from the oven and serve hot.

Seared Curried Eggplant with Spicy Yogurt Sauce

SERVES 4

These eggplant "steaks" are a treat for summer barbecues. I like to serve them over basmati rice or couscous, or in pita bread with tomato and arugula.

2 eggplants, cut lengthwise into
    1/2-inch-thick slices

Kosher salt

1/4 cup rice vinegar

3 cloves garlic

1 tablespoon peeled, chopped fresh ginger

2 shallots, chopped

1/2 cup plus 2 tablespoons vegetable oil

1/2 cup coconut milk

1 1/2 tablespoons curry powder, toasted
    (page 192)

2 teaspoons chile paste

1 teaspoon chopped cilantro

SPICY YOGURT SAUCE

2 cloves garlic, chopped

1 tablespoon peeled, chopped fresh
    ginger

1 cup plain yogurt

1 teaspoon ground toasted cumin
    seeds (page 192)

1 teaspoon chile paste plus
    additional, as needed

Soy sauce

1/4 cup olive oil

To prepare the eggplant, salt the slices and let drain on paper towels for about 10 minutes. Put the vinegar, garlic, ginger, and shallots in a medium bowl and stir. Add the oil and coconut milk and whisk to mix. Add the curry, chile paste, and cilantro and mix well. Place the eggplant in a large bowl and pour the marinade over it. Marinate for at least 30 minutes.

Meanwhile, prepare the sauce. Put the garlic, ginger, and yogurt in a medium bowl and whisk together. Add the remaining ingredients and mix well. Place in the refrigerator until ready to use.

Preheat the oven to 150°. Heat 1 tablespoon of the oil in a large nonstick sauté pan over high heat until smoking hot. Add as many eggplant slices as will fit in the pan without overcrowding. Brown the slices well on both sides until the eggplant is tender, 2 to 3 minutes per side. Transfer to a plate and place in the oven to keep warm, then repeat with the remaining eggplant. If needed, add the remaining oil during the cooking process.

Place the eggplant on a serving platter, drizzle with the sauce, and serve.

Baked Pasta with Tomato-Mushroom Sauce & Ricotta Topping

SERVES 4

This recipe is from a class I teach called, "Meals in Less Than Half an Hour." It's simple and straightforward, and kids even like it. The ricotta browns to form a nice crust. If you want to embellish the dish, sauté the zucchini and eggplant and layer it between the pasta and ricotta. You can also add cooked chicken or chorizo or chopped olives. The freshly grated Parmesan adds body and flavor. Serve this with a green salad and you'll have a beautiful meal.

TOMATO-MUSHROOM SAUCE

2 teaspoons olive oil

3 cloves garlic, chopped

1 small onion, diced

2 cups sliced wild mushrooms
(such as chanterelles and portobellos),
or button mushrooms

2 cups peeled, seeded, and diced ripe
tomatoes (page 190)

1 cup red wine

1 cup vegetable stock (page 185)

1/4 cup extra virgin olive oil

1 tablespoon chopped fresh oregano

Salt

Freshly ground black pepper

RICOTTA TOPPING

2 cups ricotta cheese

3 cloves garlic, chopped

1 head roasted garlic (page 188)

1/2 cup freshly grated Parmesan cheese

2 teaspoons chopped fresh basil

2 teaspoons chopped fresh thyme

2 teaspoons chopped fresh marjoram

Salt

Freshly ground black pepper

3/4 pound dried penne

TOMATOES

There is nothing like homegrown tomatoes. Use tomatoes at their peak, in summer. In my opinion, if tomatoes aren't fresh-picked, they aren't worth eating. You can grow tomatoes in the ground or in containers. All you need is a sunny balcony, patio, or small garden plot. If you can't grow your own, look for farm-fresh tomatoes in produce stores, and shop at farmers' markets whenever possible. We're fortunate to enjoy a great selection of tomato varieties—from brandywine and zebra (green-striped) tomatoes—compliments of our organic farmer

To prepare the sauce, place the olive oil in a large saucepan and heat over high heat until very hot. Add the garlic and onion and lightly sauté, 1 to 2 minutes. Add the mushrooms, tomatoes, and red wine and cook until the wine is reduced by about half. Add the stock and cook for about 20 minutes. Purée the sauce in the pan with a handheld blender until smooth. Alternatively, transfer to the bowl of a food processor, purée, and then return the sauce to the pan. Stir in the extra virgin olive oil and oregano. Season to taste with the salt and pepper and blend again. Set aside.

To prepare the topping, put the ricotta in a medium bowl. Add the garlic and stir well. Add the Parmesan, basil, thyme, and marjoram and mix well. Season to taste with salt and pepper and set aside.

Bring 8 cups of salted water to a boil in a stockpot. Add the penne and cook until very al dente. Drain and place in a large mixing bowl. Add the sauce and toss well. Taste and add more salt and pepper if necessary.

Preheat the oven to 350°. Butter a 9 x 13-inch baking pan. Place the pasta mixture in the baking pan and spread the ricotta topping evenly over the pasta. Bake in the oven, uncovered, for about 30 minutes, or until cooked through. Remove from the oven. Cut the pasta into squares, and serve hot.

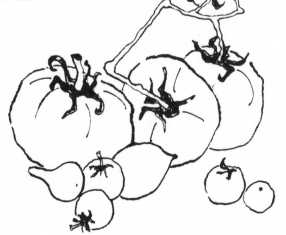

friends. If you have to use less-than-ripe tomatoes, you can roast them in a 400° oven for 25 minutes, or until they turn brown, to sweeten them up. Sometimes sundried tomatoes can be substituted for fresh, just-picked tomatoes (such as in soups).

SUNDRIED TOMATOES
I don't recommend buying oil-packed sundried tomatoes; I prefer the dry-packed ones because I want to be able to feel and see them in the package. Look for ones that are still flexible, not stiff like a piece of shoe leather that has been kiln-dried.

Stuffed Swiss Chard with Herbed Basmati & Roasted Garlic Broth

SERVES 4

This is a hip version of stuffed cabbage, one of my favorite foods. The dish is so sophisticated that no one will guess its humble origins. I love the little packages—they are appealing and tasty. I imagine the stuffed chard in a pasta plate with lots of lovely garlic broth.

8 large Swiss chard leaves
2 teaspoons olive oil
1 small bulb fennel, peeled and diced
5 cloves garlic, chopped
1/2 cup dry sherry
3 cups cooked basmati rice (page 110)
1/3 cup heavy whipping cream
1/4 cup soft fresh goat cheese
2 teaspoons Dijon mustard
1 tablespoon chopped fresh basil
1 teaspoon chopped fresh thyme
1 teaspoon chopped fresh oregano
1 teaspoon chopped fresh rosemary
Salt
Freshly ground black pepper
3 cups vegetable stock (page 185)
1 head roasted garlic (page 188)

In a large saucepan, bring 8 cups of salted water to a boil. Add the chard and cook until tender, about 5 minutes. Drain in a colander and set aside.

Heat the olive oil in medium sauté pan over high heat until very hot. Add the fennel and half of the chopped garlic and lightly sauté, 2 to 3 minutes. Add the sherry and reduce until the liquid is almost evaporated, 3 to 4 minutes. Let cool completely.

Put the rice in a medium bowl and add the cooked fennel mixture. Stir well. Add the cream and goat cheese and stir well. Add the mustard, basil, thyme, oregano, rosemary, salt, and pepper and stir well. Place about $^1/_2$ cup of filling in the center of one chard leaf. Fold the sides of the leaf around the filling, then fold the ends over the filling to form a square bundle. Set the bundle aside, seam side down, and repeat until all of the chard and filling is used.

Preheat the oven to 350°. Place the stock, roasted garlic, and the remaining chopped garlic in a large ovenproof sauté pan and bring to a boil. Season to taste with salt and pepper and then place the chard bundles seam side down in the pan. Cover with a lid and bake in the oven to heat through, 20 to 25 minutes.

To serve, place 2 chard bundles on each plate and ladle the garlic-seasoned stock over the top. Serve hot.

Vegetable Turnovers with Gorgonzola Sauce

SERVES 4

For a Christmas party I cater every year, I usually bring a seafood dish. This last year I brought baked seafood turnovers and they were a hit. This recipe is similar, except the wonderful, flaky crust is filled with savory vegetables. You can make these ahead of time and refrigerate or freeze them until you're ready to bake them. If frozen, take the turnovers straight from the freezer to the oven and add 10 minutes to the baking time.

CRUST

2 1/3 cups all-purpose flour
1/2 cup unsalted butter
1/2 cup shortening
1/2 teaspoon salt
8 tablespoons cold water

VEGETABLE FILLING

2 teaspoons olive oil
1/2 small onion, diced
2 cloves garlic, chopped
2 Yukon gold potatoes, peeled and diced
2 carrots, peeled and thinly sliced
1 cup sliced button or wild mushrooms
1 small zucchini, diced
1 cup red wine
2 teaspoons chopped fresh basil
1 teaspoon chopped fresh parsley
1 teaspoon chopped fresh thyme
Salt
Freshly ground black pepper

EGG WASH

1 egg white
1 teaspoon water

GORGONZOLA SAUCE

1 cup white wine
2 cloves garlic, chopped
2 shallots, chopped
1 cup heavy whipping cream
1/3 cup Gorgonzola cheese
Salt
Freshly ground black pepper

MUSHROOMS

When buying mushrooms, look for ones that are not dried out, wet, or curling up. Buy mushrooms with closed caps. The caps should be nice and firm. Most mushrooms are best cleaned with only a mushroom brush.

BUTTON MUSHROOMS These are also commonly known as cultivated or white mushrooms. I recommend using the more flavorful cremini or European browns whenever possible.

WILD MUSHROOMS Chanterelles, morels, oyster mushrooms,

To make the crust, place the flour, butter, shortening, and salt in a bowl. Using your fingertips, rub the mixture together until a coarse meal forms. Drizzle in the cold water and stir gently with a fork, just until the dough starts to come together. Add a bit more water if needed; it's better to have dough that is slightly wet than dough that is too dry. Cover dough in plastic wrap and let it rest for 15 to 20 minutes.

Meanwhile, prepare the filling. Heat the oil in a large sauté pan over high heat until very hot. Add the onion and garlic and lightly sauté for about 2 minutes. Add the potatoes and carrots and sauté for 4 to 5 minutes. Add the mushrooms and zucchini and lightly sauté for about 2 minutes. Add the red wine and reduce until about 2 tablespoons of liquid remain. Add the basil, parsley, and thyme and season to taste with salt and pepper. Remove from the heat and let cool completely.

Preheat the oven to 425°. Butter a baking sheet and set aside. Place the dough on a well-floured work surface and roll it out into a 24-inch square. Cut the square into 4 equal squares. Distribute the cooled vegetable filling evenly in the center of the 4 squares. Fold a corner of the dough over the filling to form a triangle shape, and crimp the edges with the tines of a fork to seal well.

To make the egg wash, whisk together the egg white and water. Using a pastry brush, coat the top of the turnovers with the egg mixture. Place the turnovers on the prepared baking sheet and place the pan in the oven. Bake for about 20 minutes, or until golden brown.

Meanwhile, prepare the sauce. Place the wine, garlic, and shallots in a medium sauté pan over high heat and reduce until about 1/4 cup of liquid remains. Add the cream and reduce again over high heat until about 1/2 cup of liquid remains and the sauce is thickened. Add the Gorgonzola. Season to taste with salt and pepper.

Remove the turnovers from the oven, and let them cool for a minute on the baking sheet. Using a metal spatula, transfer the turnovers to a serving platter or individual plates. Pour the sauce over the top and serve hot.

shiitakes, portobellos, and porcini are wild mushrooms I like to use in many dishes. We are fortunate in the Northwest because fresh wild mushrooms are becoming increasingly available. Many supermarkets carry wild mushrooms in the produce section. If fresh wild mushrooms are not available, I recommend using button mushrooms in combination with dried wild mushrooms, such as porcini or shiitakes, reconstituted with water. If you reconstitute dried mushrooms, you can add the soaking liquid to the dish.

Roasted Delicata Squash with Garlic, Cheese & Toasted Nut Stuffing

SERVES 4

NUTS

I suggest lightly toasting nuts before using them in any dish because it intensifies their nuttiness and unique flavors.

ALMONDS

The almond is a delicate nut with a subtle but distinctive flavor. It can be ground and used to coat pan-fried fish or incorporated into the crust of a lemon tart.

HAZELNUTS

I usually remove the slightly bitter skins after toasting (for toasting and skinning instructions, see page 191) to be sure they don't alter the flavor of the dish.

Delicatas are my favorite winter squash. They are narrow with green and white stripes and have just the right amount of richness. I started using delicatas when we began buying specialty vegetables from organic farmers. At the Bistro, we stuff the squash with a meat filling, but this vegetarian stuffing is equally delicious. You can substitute acorn squash if you prefer.

2 small delicata squash,
   halved crosswise and
   centers scooped out
Salt
Freshly ground black pepper
Extra virgin olive oil

STUFFING

2 teaspoons olive oil
1/2 onion, minced
3 cloves garlic, chopped
2 stalks celery, finely diced
1/2 cup dry sherry
2 cups diced French bread
1/2 to 3/4 cup vegetable stock (page 185)
2 eggs, lightly beaten
1 cup ground toasted hazelnuts (page 191)
1/2 cup ground toasted pecans (page 191)
1 tablespoon chopped fresh thyme
2 teaspoons chopped fresh sage
1/2 teaspoon salt
1 teaspoon freshly ground black pepper

Preheat the oven to 350°. To prepare the squash, place it cut-side up in a roasting pan, sprinkle salt and pepper over it, and drizzle the oil over the top. Bake in the oven for 35 to 40 minutes.

Meanwhile, prepare the stuffing. Heat the olive oil in a medium sauté pan until very hot. Add the onion, garlic, and celery and sauté for about 3 minutes. Add the sherry and cook over high heat until reduced by half. Remove from the heat and let cool completely. When the onion mixture is cool, transfer it to a medium bowl and add the diced French bread. Toss to mix. Add enough of the stock to soften the bread, and then add the eggs and stir to mix well. Add the hazelnuts, pecans, thyme, sage, salt, and pepper and stir to mix well. Set aside.

Remove the squash from the oven. Without removing the squash from the pan, divide the filling among each half, spooning it into the scooped out cavities, and return the pan to the oven. Bake for 30 minutes, or until the stuffing is hot all the way through. Remove from the oven.

To serve, place the squash halves on a large serving platter or on individual plates. Serve hot.

Hazelnuts have a strong flavor, so don't use them in delicate dishes. They make the perfect addition to green salads with robust dressings or in wild mushroom pasta dishes.

MACADAMIA NUTS

These Hawaiian nuts are rich with a very subtle flavor. They are most often used in desserts, but can add texture to savory dishes as well.

PECANS

Often used in desserts, the pecan is a sweet, rich nut.

Summer Risotto with Corn, Asparagus & Fresh Basil

SERVES 4

This is what I make for supper when I am home by myself. If the kids are home, I add only corn at first. Then after I've served them, I add the other sauteed veggies to the remainder of the risotto for me.

1 tablespoon olive oil

3 cloves garlic

2 shallots, chopped

2 cups arborio rice

1 quart roasted vegetable stock, heated just until boiling (page 185)

1 pound asparagus, cut on the diagonal

3 vine-ripened plum tomatoes, cored and diced

2 tablespoons chopped fresh basil, some tops reserved for garnish

Kernels from 3 ears of corn (about 1 1/2 cups)

3/4 cup freshly grated Parmesan cheese

Salt

Freshly ground black pepper

Zest of 1 lemon, for garnish

2 tablespoons extra virgin olive oil

Heat the olive oil in a large saucepan over high heat until very hot. Add the garlic and shallots and sauté until fragrant, about 1 minute. Add the rice and sauté for about 2 minutes to toast. Add enough of the stock to cover the rice and cook, stirring constantly. When the stock has been absorbed, add more hot stock. Repeat the process until the rice is very al dente, 10 to 12 minutes. When the rice is just al dente, about 5 minutes, add the asparagus, tomatoes, and basil. If needed, add more stock. When the last stock has been absorbed, add the corn and about 1/2 cup of the Parmesan cheese and mix well. Season to taste with salt and pepper and place in a large serving bowl or on individual plates. Sprinkle the remaining 1/4 cup of Parmesan cheese, the lemon zest, olive oil, and reserved fresh basil over the top and serve hot.

Pappardelle with Walnut-Herb Sauce

SERVES 4

This is a fresh, uncooked sauce, perfect for hot weather. If you have an herb garden, here's a good reason to raid it. I use the pappardelle noodles because I love their generous width and the extra body they add to this vegetarian dish, but you may substitute any other wide noodle.

WALNUT-HERB SAUCE
1 cup walnuts, toasted (page 191)
1/2 cup freshly grated Parmesan cheese
3 cloves garlic
1/3 cup packed fresh thyme leaves
1/3 cup packed fresh basil leaves
1/4 cup packed fresh marjoram
2/3 cup extra virgin olive oil
Salt
1 teaspoon cracked black pepper

1 pound fresh pappardelle
2/3 cup freshly grated Parmesan cheese

To prepare the sauce, place the walnuts, Parmesan, garlic, and herbs in the bowl of a food processor fitted with the metal blade and process until coarsely chopped. With the motor running, slowly add the olive oil through the feeder tube. Process until the sauce is smooth. Season to taste with the salt and pepper. Transfer to a large mixing bowl, and set aside.

To prepare the pasta, bring 8 cups of salted water to a rolling boil in a stockpot. Add the pasta and cook just until the water returns to a boil, occasionally stirring to keep the noodles separated. Drain the pasta, add them to the bowl of sauce, and toss well.

To serve, place the pasta on a serving platter or on individual pasta plates and top with the grated cheese. Serve immediately.

Braised White Beans with Wild Mushrooms & Goat Cheese

SERVES 4

I often have a bowl of braised white beans with lots of rosemary and garlic for dinner. Adding wild mushrooms, crumbled goat cheese, and fresh herbs makes it even more delicious and satisfying. When you stir in the goat cheese, it melts slightly and adds tang and creaminess to the dish.

2 cups dried cannellini beans
10 cups vegetable stock (page 185)
1 tablespoon olive oil
1 onion, julienned
3 cloves garlic, chopped
3 cups sliced wild mushrooms (such as chanterelles and portobellos)
2 cups red wine
2 ripe tomatoes, cored, seeded, and diced
1 tablespoon chopped fresh rosemary
2 teaspoons chopped fresh thyme
2 teaspoons chopped fresh basil
1 tablespoon unsalted butter
Salt
Freshly ground black pepper
4 ounces soft mild goat cheese, crumbled

BEANS

I used to think a bean was a bean. Then I tasted a cannellini bean and discovered the difference between beans can be remarkable. Beans are low in fat, high in protein, and all-around good for us. They add a satisfying depth and texture to stews and soups. To properly cook dried beans, soak them overnight in cold water. The next day, rinse and cook them in unsalted water. Drain, then use or store in the refrigerator for up to 2 days.

There are many types of beans available, and most taste better than the pinto and great northern beans that Americans have traditionally used.

Place the beans in a large container, cover with cold water, and place in the refrigerator overnight.

Drain the beans, place them in a large stockpot, and cover with 8 cups of the stock. Cook until tender, about 20 minutes. Drain the beans in a colander and set aside.

Heat the olive oil in a large sauté pan over high heat until very hot. Add the onion and garlic and sauté until fragrant, about 2 minutes. Add the mushrooms and sauté for 4 to 5 minutes, or until the mushrooms are tender. Add the red wine and reduce until about $1/2$ cup remains. Add the beans, tomatoes, and the remaining 2 cups of stock and bring to a boil. Add the thyme and basil and cook for about 5 minutes. Add the butter and season to taste with salt and pepper.

To serve, divide the beans among 4 pasta bowls and top with the goat cheese. Serve hot.

Here are a few of my favorites:

BLACK BEANS
Commonly used in Mexican food, black beans add color and flavor to salsas and soups.

CANNELLINI BEANS
Whenever a recipe calls for white beans, use these. They have more flavor and are smaller and lower in starch than great northerns.

CRANBERRY BEANS
These beans also have a low starch content. They are sweet and can be substituted for white beans.

FLAGEOLETS
These tiny, green beans are delicate and also low in starch.

Roasted Tomatoes Stuffed with Fresh Herbs & a Trio of Cheeses

SERVES 6

As with all tomato recipes, you need to make this when tomatoes are in season and at their prime. The tomatoes go very nicely with penne pasta tossed with a garlicky cream sauce.

6 large beefsteak tomatoes
2 cloves garlic, minced
1 cup toasted unseasoned bread crumbs
1/2 cup grated Gouda cheese
1/3 cup freshly grated Parmesan cheese
1/2 cup cream cheese
2 tablespoons chopped fresh basil
2 tablespoons olive oil
1 teaspoon dry mustard powder
2 tablespoons chopped dry-packed sundried tomatoes
Salt
Freshly ground black pepper

Using a sharp knife, cut the top off each tomato. Without breaking through the skin, carefully scoop out the inside of the tomato with a melon baller or a spoon and discard. Set the tomato shells aside.

Preheat the oven to 350°. Put the garlic, bread crumbs, Gouda, Parmesan, cream cheese, basil, olive oil, mustard, and sundried tomatoes in a medium bowl and mix well. Season to taste with salt and pepper and mix well again. Spoon the filling into the tomatoes, dividing it evenly, and place the tomatoes upright in a roasting pan. Bake in the oven until the cheese is hot and the tops are golden brown, 20 to 25 minutes. Remove from the oven and serve hot.

Risotto-Style Toasted Barley with Parmesan & Grilled Bell Peppers

SERVES 4

I once had a delicious toasted barley risotto at a restaurant in Toronto, and decided to try my hand at re-creating it. Risotto made with arborio rice can be heavy in summer, so the light, slightly nutty barley is a nice substitute. It's also a good opportunity to use a somewhat overlooked grain. You can grill or sauté the peppers. This "risotto" would also be good with chunks of grilled chicken or fresh corn kernels added in.

2 tablespoons unsalted butter

1 small onion, diced

3 cloves garlic, chopped

2 cups pearl barley

5 cups hot vegetable stock (page 185)

2 red bell peppers, roasted, peeled, seeded, and diced (page 190)

2 yellow bell peppers, roasted peeled, seeded, and diced (page 190)

2 teaspoons chopped fresh sage

2 teaspoons chopped fresh rosemary

Salt

Freshly ground black pepper

1 cup freshly shaved Parmesan cheese

Heat the butter in a large saucepan over high heat until very hot. Add the onion and garlic and lightly sauté, about 3 minutes. Add the pearl barley and toast for about 2 minutes, stirring constantly. Stir in about 3 cups of the stock and cook until all of the liquid is absorbed, 5 to 7 minutes. Add the red and the yellow bell peppers and the remaining stock and cook, stirring periodically, for 3 to 5 minutes. Add the sage and rosemary and cook until the barley is just tender, another 3 to 5 minutes. Season to taste with salt and black pepper.

To serve, mound the barley risotto on a large serving platter. Top with the shaved Parmesan and serve hot.

Polenta & Pesto Lasagne

SERVES 6

You could make this with any kind of pesto—basil, sundried tomato, or red bell pepper. I keep it simple, so the polenta's natural flavor isn't overwhelmed.

POLENTA

6 cups vegetable stock (page 185)

4 cloves garlic, chopped

3 shallots, chopped

2 tablespoons Durkee's cayenne sauce

3 cups finely ground cornmeal

2 tablespoons unsalted butter

1 teaspoon salt

1 teaspoon freshly ground black pepper

PESTO

3 cups fresh basil leaves

4 cloves garlic

1 cup pine nuts or walnuts, toasted (page 191)

1 cup freshly grated Parmesan

3/4 cup extra virgin olive oil

2 cups ricotta cheese

2 cups blue cheese

1 cup freshly grated Parmesan

To prepare the polenta, butter a 9 x 11-inch baking pan. Heat the stock, garlic, shallots, and cayenne sauce in a medium saucepan until it reaches a rolling boil. While whisking, slowly add the cornmeal in a thin stream. Cook over medium heat, stirring until very thick, about 5 minutes. Add the butter and season with salt and pepper. Pour into the prepared pan and set aside to cool.

To prepare the pesto, put the basil, garlic, nuts, and Parmesan in the bowl of a food processor and process until the mixture is smooth. Scrape down the sides of the bowl and, with the machine running, slowly add the olive oil through the feeder tube. Purée until smooth. Transfer the pesto to a bowl and set aside.

To make the lasagne, preheat the oven to 350°. Run the blade of a knife around the edge of the polenta to loosen it from the pan. Gently invert the pan and remove the cooled polenta. With a long-bladed, sharp knife, cut the polenta into two equal sheets. Place one layer of the polenta in the baking pan. Spread half of the pesto on the polenta. Spread about half of the ricotta on top of the pesto. Sprinkle half of the blue cheese and Parmesan cheese over the ricotta. Place the other half of polenta on top of the cheese. Cover with the remaining cheese. Bake in the oven for 30 minutes, or until the cheese is melted and hot. Remove the lasagne from the oven and let cool for 3 to 4 minutes. Cut into portions, transfer to individual plates and serve.

Asian-Style Ravioli in Coconut-Curry Broth

SERVES 4

I love dumplings of every size, shape, and type, and these are some of my favorites. The ravioli can be made ahead, pre-frozen on a baking sheet, and then stored in the freezer. To cook them, just drop the frozen ravioli into a saucepan of boiling water.

FILLING

1 tablespoon peeled, chopped fresh ginger

2 cloves garlic

3 green onions, cut into thirds

1 large carrot, peeled and cut into chunks

6 snow peas

1 red bell pepper, cut into chunks

1/2 cup shiitake mushrooms, sliced

2 teaspoons vegetable oil

1 teaspoon sesame oil

1 teaspoon chile sauce

Soy sauce

48 wonton wrappers

COCONUT-CURRY BROTH

2 teaspoons vegetable oil

2 cloves garlic, chopped

2 teaspoons peeled, chopped
   fresh ginger

3/4 cup vegetable stock (page 185)

1 1/4 cups coconut milk

2 teaspoons honey

1 tablespoon curry powder, toasted
   (page 192)

1 teaspoon chile paste

1 teaspoon chopped cilantro

Soy sauce

4 sprigs parsley, snipped

To prepare the ravioli filling, place the ginger, garlic, and all of the vegetables in the bowl of a food processor fitted with the metal blade and pulse to coarsely chop. Heat the vegetable oil in a medium sauté pan until very hot. Add the vegetables and sauté for 3 to 4 minutes. Add the remaining filling ingredients and stir well. Remove from the heat and set aside to cool completely.

To prepare the ravioli, place 1 of the wonton wrappers on a work surface. Place a heaping teaspoon of filling in the center of the wrapper and brush the edges of the wrapper with water. Place a second wrapper on top of the mixture and press the edges together to seal. Repeat with the remaining filling and wrappers. Set aside.

To prepare the broth, heat the oil in a large sauté pan over high heat until very hot. Add the garlic and ginger and quickly sauté, about 1 minute. Add the stock,

continued

Asian-Style Ravioli *continued*

coconut milk, and honey and bring to a boil. Add the curry powder, chile paste, and cilantro. Decrease the heat to medium and simmer for about 10 minutes.

Bring 8 cups of salted water to a boil in a large saucepan. Add the ravioli and let the water return to a boil. Drain the ravioli in a colander and add to the broth. Season the broth to taste with soy sauce.

Distribute the ravioli among 4 large, shallow bowls. Ladle some of the broth over the top, garnish with the parsley, and serve hot.

Wild Mushroom–Potato Gratin

SERVES 4

Roasted potatoes and mushrooms are a perfect pair. Use Yukon golds or yellow Finns for the most flavorful results. I like to serve this as a main dish with a spinach salad on the side.

2 tablespoons olive oil

1 1/2 pounds wild mushrooms (such as chanterelles and portobellos), sliced

3 cloves garlic, chopped

1 onion, julienned

1 tablespoon chopped fresh parsley

2 teaspoons chopped fresh rosemary

1 cup freshly grated Parmesan cheese

1 cup heavy whipping cream

1 pound Yukon gold potatoes, peeled and thinly sliced

1 cup roasted vegetable stock (page 185)

Pinch of salt

1 teaspoon cracked black pepper

Preheat the oven to 350°. Heat the olive oil in a Dutch oven over high heat. Add the mushrooms and sauté until tender, 3 to 4 minutes. Add the garlic, onion, parsley, and rosemary and lightly sauté, about 2 minutes. Remove the pan from the heat and sprinkle half of the cheese and pour half the cream over the mushrooms. Place the potato slices on top of the mushrooms and pour the stock over the potatoes. Add the remaining cheese and cream and sprinkle with salt and pepper. Bake in the oven until the potatoes are tender, 40 to 50 minutes. Serve hot out of the Dutch oven.

Desserts

Pecan-Pumpkin Cake
with White Chocolate–Ginger Mousse

SERVES 12

I had a very plain pumpkin pudding cake once that inspired my imagination. I'm always looking for new and interesting ways to remake old favorites, like pumpkin pie. So, I started experimenting. I discovered that white chocolate is absolutely delicious with pumpkin and the soft pudding texture of the cake is delightful. I like to serve this cake during the holidays. Kids love it, too.

PUMPKIN CAKE

2 cups canned pumpkin purée

1 1/2 cups sugar

1 cup pecans, toasted (page 191)

3/4 cup all-purpose flour

3 whole eggs

3 eggs, separated

1 teaspoon pure vanilla extract

2 teaspoons ground cinnamon

1 teaspoon allspice

1 teaspoon ground nutmeg

1 teaspoon ground ginger

WHITE CHOCOLATE–GINGER MOUSSE

10 ounces white chocolate

1/4 cup unsalted butter

5 egg yolks

3/4 cup sugar

1/3 cup dark rum

1/4 cup chopped candied ginger

1 cup heavy whipping cream

1 teaspoon pure vanilla extract

Ground cinnamon

To prepare the cake, preheat the oven to 350°. Butter a 9-inch springform pan, and set aside. Put the pumpkin purée, sugar, pecans, and flour in a large bowl and mix well. Add the whole eggs and egg yolks and mix well to blend. Add the vanilla, cinnamon, allspice, nutmeg, and ginger, and mix well. Put the egg whites in a medium bowl and whip with a handheld beater until soft peaks form, or use a heavy-duty electric mixer to whip. Gently fold the egg whites into the pumpkin mixture. Pour the batter into the prepared pan and bake in the oven for 30 to 40 minutes, or until a knife inserted in the center of the cake comes out clean. Remove from the oven and set aside to cool completely.

To prepare the mousse, put the chocolate and butter in the top of a double boiler and bring to a slow simmer to slowly melt the white chocolate. Meanwhile, put the eggs, sugar, rum, and 2 tablespoons of ginger in a medium metal bowl and whisk together. Set the bowl in a saucepan of simmering water and whisk the mixture until it is thick and resembles softly whipped cream, about 4 minutes. Be careful not to let the eggs get too hot (or they will scramble). Fold the melted white chocolate into the egg mixture. Place the mixture in the refrigerator for 30 to 45 minutes to chill.

To assemble the cake, remove the mousse from the refrigerator. Put the cream and the vanilla in a medium metal bowl and whip with a handheld beater until soft peaks form. Gently fold the whipped cream into the mousse. Pour this mixture over the top of the pumpkin cake and let it set for 2 to 4 hours in the refrigerator before serving.

To serve, slice the cake into wedges. Top each slice with a bit of candied ginger and a sprinkling of cinnamon.

Decadent Double-Chocolate Brownie Torte

SERVES 10

You'll have your guests on their knees with this dessert. The torte takes about fifteen minutes to put together and thirty minutes to bake, which makes it great for drop-in company or for those winter evenings when dessert just sounds so good! I like to serve the warm, gooey brownie with whipped cream and fresh raspberries or a scoop of vanilla ice cream drizzled with warm caramel or chocolate sauce.

5 ounces unsweetened chocolate
1/2 cup unsalted butter
1 1/2 cups sugar
4 large eggs
1 teaspoon pure vanilla extract
1/4 cup all-purpose flour
2 ounces bittersweet chocolate, chopped
3 ounces white chocolate, chopped
1/4 cup finely ground toasted pecans (page 191)
1 cup heavy whipping cream, or 1 quart vanilla ice cream
Seasonal berries

CHOCOLATE

Chocolate is made from the cocoa bean THEOBROMA CACAO, and was dubbed the food of the gods by the Aztecs, the Americas' first chocoholics. In the fifteenth century, Montezuma, the last Aztec emperor of Mexico, is said to have drunk fifty goblets of it a day because he thought it was an aphrodisiac.

Chocolate is processed and sold in various forms. After the beans are removed from the pods, they're fermented, dried, roasted, and cracked, separating the nibs (which contain 54 percent cocoa butter) from the shells. The nibs are ground to extract some of the

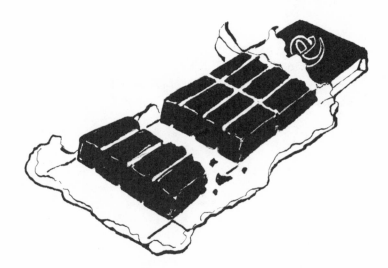

To prepare the cake, preheat the oven to 350°. Line the bottom of a 9-inch cake pan with parchment paper and set aside.

Put the unsweetened chocolate and butter in a metal bowl and place it in the top of a double boiler over slowly simmering water until the chocolate is melted. Place the sugar and eggs in the bowl of a heavy-duty mixer and whip on high speed for about 5 minutes, or until a pale lemony color and thick. Decrease the speed to medium and slowly add the melted chocolate mixture. Scrape down the sides of the bowl and add the vanilla. Gradually add the flour, mixing just until the batter comes together. Remove the bowl from the mixer and set aside for about 5 minutes to let the batter cool slightly.

Fold the chopped bittersweet chocolate, white chocolate, and pecans into the batter and pour the batter into the prepared pan. Place the pan in the oven and bake until a knife inserted in the center of the cake comes out clean, 30 to 35 minutes. Remove the cake from the oven and cool in the pan for about 10 minutes. Meanwhile, whip the cream to soft peaks.

To remove the cake from the pan, run a knife around the inside edge of the pan, then invert the cake onto a platter. Cut into individual portions and serve warm or at room temperature with the whipped cream or vanilla ice cream, and top with the berries.

cocoa butter, leaving a thick brown paste called chocolate liquor. Next, the liquor is refined. If additional cocoa butter is extracted from the liquor, the solid result is ground to produce unsweetened cocoa powder. If other ingredients are added, such as milk powder or sugar, the chocolate is refined again. The final step for most chocolate is called conching. Huge machines with rotating blades blend the heated chocolate liquor, ridding it of residual moisture and volatile acids. The conching process takes 12 to 72 hours (depending on the type and quality of chocolate), during which small amounts of cocoa butter and sometimes lecithin are added to make the chocolate smooth.

White Chocolate–Raspberry Roulade

SERVES 12

A roulade is a light cake that is rolled around a filling. This is a light dessert, but in no way will you feel cheated out of a sinful splurge. The simple cake is filled with a mixture of melted white chocolate, ricotta cheese, and fresh raspberries and then covered with dark chocolate. I've also made this cake with fresh strawberries or blackberries instead of the raspberries, and I've made it without berries at all. I like to cover the cake with whipped cream or cocoa powder.

CAKE

6 whole eggs
1 egg yolk
1/2 cup granulated sugar
1/2 teaspoon almond extract
1/2 cup all-purpose flour
1/2 cup confectioners' sugar

FILLING

6 ounces white chocolate
2 cups ricotta cheese
1/2 cup heavy whipping cream
Zest of 1 orange
1 teaspoon vanilla extract
3 cups fresh raspberries

TOPPING

12 ounces bittersweet chocolate
1 1/4 cups heavy whipping cream
4 ounces white chocolate

To prepare the cake, preheat the oven to 350°. Spray a jelly-roll pan with vegetable oil cooking spray. Line the bottom of the pan with parchment paper and spray the paper with cooking spray. Set aside.

Place 3 of the whole eggs in the bowl of a heavy-duty electric mixer. Separate the remaining 3 eggs, adding the yolks to the bowl with the whole eggs and placing the whites in a separate bowl. Add the additional egg yolk to the bowl with the whole eggs. Add the sugar and almond extract and whip on high speed until the mixture is thickened and a lemon yellow color, about 5 minutes. Remove the bowl from the mixer and gently fold in the all-purpose flour, using large strokes. Place the bowl with the egg whites on the mixer and whip on high speed until they hold a soft peak. Gently fold the whites into the egg mixture and pour into the prepared pan. Place the pan in the oven and bake for about 20 minutes, or until golden brown and the cake springs back when lightly pressed with a fingertip. Remove the cake from the oven and let cool for about 5 minutes.

Loosen the cake from the pan with a knife or spatula. Dust a clean kitchen towel with the confectioners' sugar and invert the cake onto the towel. Gently roll the cake into a log, using the kitchen towel to guide and support it. The cake can be made ahead up to this point and kept overnight covered in plastic wrap at room temperature.

To prepare the filling, melt the white chocolate slowly in the top of a double boiler over gently simmering water. When the chocolate is melted, fold it into the ricotta cheese. Add the whipping cream, orange zest, and vanilla and fold in the raspberries. Mix well. Unroll the cake and place it on a work surface. Spread the filling evenly over the cake. Gently roll up the cake jelly-roll style and place it on a baking sheet lined with parchment paper. Refrigerate the cake until ready to glaze.

To prepare the topping, place the bittersweet chocolate pieces in the bowl of a food processor and process until the chocolate is finely chopped. Put the cream in a small saucepan and heat just until it comes to a boil. With the machine running, pour the hot cream into the food processor through the feeder tube and process until very smooth. Allow the mixture to cool until thick, 20 to 30 minutes. Meanwhile, melt the white chocolate in the top of a double boiler over gently simmering water. Pour the chocolate-cream mixture over the cake. Drizzle with the melted white chocolate and refrigerate, uncovered, until ready to serve.

To serve, slice with a serrated knife into $^1/2$ - to 1-inch-thick pieces.

Chocolate should be stored tightly wrapped in a cool, dry place (60° to 70°). Chocolate should be melted slowly over low heat in the top of a double boiler over simmering water. Remove the top pan from the heat when the chocolate is a little more than halfway melted and stir until completely smooth. Chocolate can be melted with liquid added (at least $^1/4$ cup liquid per 6 ounces chocolate). But a single drop of water added to melted chocolate will cause it to clump and harden in the pan. This may be corrected if vegetable oil is stirred into the chocolate at a ratio of 1 tablespoon oil to 6 ounces of chocolate. Slowly re-melt the mixture and stir again until smooth.

Strawberry-Chocolate Linzertorte

SERVES 12

This is another of my twists on a classic dessert. The traditional linzertorte has a nut dough with lots of cinnamon and a jam filling. This is a classic linzer dough, with pecans and cinnamon, but I use fresh strawberries and chunks of chocolate for the filling instead of jam. It can be served warm or cold. When I serve the torte warm, I like to serve a scoop of ice cream on the side. If I'm serving the torte cold, a warm chocolate sauce drizzled over the top is a great addition. When strawberries are at their peak in summer, this is a perfect dessert.

DOUGH

2 cups all-purpose flour

1 cup sugar

2 cups pecans

1 cup unsalted butter

2 eggs

1 teaspoon ground cinnamon

1 teaspoon pure vanilla extract

FILLING

5 cups hulled and quartered strawberries (about 7 cups whole berries)

3/4 cup sugar

2 tablespoons cornstarch

Zest of 1 lemon

1/2 teaspoon ground ginger

1/2 teaspoon allspice

Pinch of ground cinnamon

4 ounces bittersweet chocolate, cut in pieces

To prepare the dough, butter a 10-inch springform pan. Put the flour, sugar, and pecans in the bowl of a food processor and process until you have a fine meal. With the machine running, add the butter through the feeder tube 1 tablespoon at a time. Stop the machine and scrape down the sides of the bowl. Add the eggs, cinnamon, and vanilla and process until a soft dough forms. Transfer the dough to a medium bowl, cover with plastic wrap, and refrigerate for at least 30 minutes. Press half of the dough into the prepared pan and refrigerate it until ready to fill. Reserve the remaining dough in the refrigerator for the top of the tart.

To prepare the tart, preheat the oven to 350°. Put the strawberries, sugar, cornstarch, zest, ginger, allspice, cinnamon, and chocolate in a large mixing bowl and stir to combine. Remove the prepared crust from the refrigerator and pour the filling into it. Crumble the reserved dough over the top, covering it evenly. Put the torte in the oven and bake for 35 to 45 minutes, or until the crust is golden brown. Remove from the oven and set aside to cool slightly before slicing, about 10 minutes.

Cut into wedges and serve warm, or refrigerate and serve chilled.

Frozen Caramelized Pear Torte

SERVES 12

The soft mousse and rich, sweet caramelized pears sandwiched between the crispy meringue layers make this a dessert a textural indulgence.

PEARS

Here in pear country, we have the luxury of eating and cooking many different varieties in even more ways. Pears are delicious fresh, dried, baked, and poached. For recipes that call for poaching or baking pears, use firm, ripe pears so they will still hold their shape and not turn mushy when cooked. (Ripe pears are best for adding to salads

ALMOND MERINGUE

6 egg whites

1 cup granulated sugar

1 teaspoon almond extract

1/2 cup ground toasted almonds (page 191)

1/2 cup flour

1/2 cup confectioners' sugar

WHITE CHOCOLATE–PEAR MOUSSE

5 ounces white chocolate

6 egg yolks

1 cup sugar

1/4 cup dark rum

2 cups heavy whipping cream

2 pears, peeled and diced

WHITE CHOCOLATE GANACHE

12 ounces white chocolate

1 cup cream

To prepare the meringue, draw two 10-inch circles on two parchment paper–lined baking sheets, then flip over the parchment so the ink is on the other side. Place the egg whites in bowl of a mixer and whip on high speed until soft peaks form. Slowly add the sugar about 1 tablespoon at a time, along with the almond extract, and whip until stiff peaks form and the whites are shiny. Place the ground almonds, flour, and confectioners' sugar in a bowl and mix together. Gently fold the mixture into the egg whites. Divide the batter between the two circles and spread evenly to fill the circles. Place in a 300° oven and bake for about 2 hours, or until firm.

To prepare the mousse, melt the white chocolate in the top of a double boiler over gently simmering heat. Transfer to a small mixing bowl. Place the egg yolks, $^3/_4$ cup of the sugar, and the rum in a metal bowl and whisk together. Place over gently simmering water, and whip the egg mixture until it is thick and resembles softly whipped cream. Remove from the heat and set aside. Whip the cream to soft peaks. Fold the whipped cream into the egg mixture, then fold in the melted white chocolate. Place in the refrigerator until ready to use.

Place the remaining 1/4 cup of sugar in a sauté pan and cook, without stirring, until the sugar turns golden brown. Add the pears and sauté until tender, 3 to 5 minutes. Set aside.

To assemble the torte, place one of the cooled meringues in a 10-inch spring-form pan. (You may have to trim the meringue fit it in the pan.) Place the pears on top of the first meringue layer, then cover with the mousse. Place the second layer of meringue on top of the mousse and place in the freezer.

To prepare the ganache, place the white chocolate pieces in the food processor and process until finely ground. Heat the cream until boiling and pour over the chocolate through the feed tube while the processor is running. Continue to process until the mixture is smooth. Remove the torte from the freezer and pour the ganache over the torte. Return the torte to the freezer and freeze for about 2 hours. (If frozen overnight, let the torte come to room temperature for about 20 minutes before cutting and serving.) To serve, release the sides of the pan and slide the torte off the bottom of the pan onto a serving platter. Slice into wedges and serve.

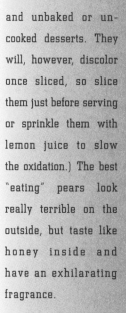

and unbaked or un-cooked desserts. They will, however, discolor once sliced, so slice them just before serving or sprinkle them with lemon juice to slow the oxidation.) The best "eating" pears look really terrible on the outside, but taste like honey inside and have an exhilarating fragrance.

John's Lemon Curd & Blueberry Cheesecake

SERVES 12

One day, John had half a recipe of lemon curd left over, so he spread a layer of it on top of a small cheesecake. We've been serving it ever since!

CRUST

2 cups all-purpose flour

1/2 cup firmly packed brown sugar

1 teaspoon pure vanilla extract

Pinch of salt

1 cup unsalted butter, diced

FILLING

1 pound cream cheese

3/4 cup sugar

3 eggs

Dash of pure vanilla extract

3/4 cup blueberries, huckleberries, or other seasonal berries

LEMON CURD

1/2 cup freshly squeezed lemon juice

Zest of 1 lemon

1 1/4 cups sugar

4 eggs

1 egg yolk

1/2 cup unsalted butter, diced

1 cup heavy whipping cream

Blueberry Sauce (page 192)

To prepare the crust, preheat the oven to 350°. Put the flour, sugar, vanilla, and salt in the bowl of a food processor. With the motor running, add the butter through the feeder tube and process until a smooth dough forms. Press the dough into a 10-inch springform pan and bake for 10 minutes, or until the dough is set. Remove from the oven and set aside to cool.

To prepare the filling, put the cream cheese, sugar, and eggs into the bowl of the food processor and process until smooth. Add the vanilla and process just to mix. Pour the mixture into a large bowl, stir in the berries, and pour the mixture into the prepared crust. Bake in the oven until the cheesecake is set, 45 minutes to 1 hour. Remove from the oven and set aside to cool, at least 30 minutes.

To prepare the lemon curd, put the juice, zest, sugar, and eggs in a metal bowl, and mix well. Add the butter and place the bowl over a pan of gently simmering water. Cook, stirring often, until the mixture is very thick and coats the back of a spoon, 5 to 8 minutes. Set the bowl aside to cool. Pour the curd over the cooled cheesecake. Refrigerate for 2 hours.

Whip the cream to soft peaks. Slice the cheesecake and serve with blueberry sauce and a dollop of the whipped cream.

Chocolate Truffle Tart
with Pecan-Caramel Sauce

SERVES 12

The base of this dessert is a crisp chocolate crust with a gooey brownie filling. A sea of Pecan-Caramel Sauce is poured over the whole lovely picture. Serve this warm, just out of the oven—you won't be able to wait.

CRUST

1 2/3 cups all-purpose flour

1/3 cup cocoa powder

3/4 cup confectioners' sugar

1 teaspoon pure vanilla extract

1/2 teaspoon ground cinnamon

1/2 teaspoon salt

1 cup unsalted butter

FILLING

1/2 cup unsalted butter

1 pound bittersweet chocolate, cut in pieces

1/2 cup sugar

4 eggs

1 teaspoon pure vanilla extract

1 heaping tablespoon instant espresso powder

SAUCE

1 cup sugar

1/3 cup water

1 1/2 cup coarsely chopped pecans

1/3 cup light Karo syrup

1/2 cup heavy whipping cream

1/4 cup dark rum

2 tablespoons unsalted butter

1 cup heavy heavy whipping cream, or 1 quart vanilla ice cream

4 sprigs mint

To prepare the crust, preheat the oven to 350°. Butter a 10-inch flan or tart pan with a removable bottom and set aside.

Put the flour, cocoa powder, confectioners' sugar, vanilla, cinnamon, and salt in the bowl of a food processor. With the machine running, add the butter about 1 tablespoon at a time through the feeder tube. Process until the dough collects on top of the blade. Remove the dough from the processor bowl and press it into the prepared pan. Bake in the oven for about 10 minutes, or just until the dough is set. Remove from the oven and let cool. Do not turn off the oven.

To prepare the filling, put the butter and half of the chocolate pieces in the top of a double boiler over the gently simmering water and melt the chocolate

continued

Chocolate Truffle Tart *continued*

completely. Remove the bowl from the heat and stir in the sugar and eggs. Mix well. Add the remaining chocolate pieces, the vanilla, and the espresso powder and mix well. Pour the filling into the prepared crust and bake in the oven for about 30 minutes, or just until the middle is set. Meanwhile, make the sauce.

To prepare the sauce, place the sugar in a large sauté pan and gently moisten with the water. Cook over high heat for 5 to 6 minutes. Do not stir. When the caramel starts to turn golden, swirl the pan to even the color of the caramel. Add the pecans and Karo syrup and then add the cream slowly. Cook until the sugar dissolves and the sauce starts to thicken, 3 to 5 minutes. Add the rum and butter and cook until the butter is melted, about 1 minute. Remove the pan from the heat and let the sauce cool for about 15 minutes. (If you make the sauce ahead, rewarm it before serving.)

If serving the tart with whipped cream, whip the cream to soft peaks. Slice the tart while it is still warm. Pour some of the hot sauce over each slice, top with a dollop of whipped cream or a scoop of ice cream, garnish with mint, and serve.

Espresso-Rum Crème Brûlée

SERVES 6

The Bistro is known for its desserts, and the crème brûlée is a regular on the menu. There are two ways to cook brûlées: on the stovetop and in the oven. After experimenting with both, I prefer the texture of the oven-baked brûlées. If you make brûlées regularly, you should invest in a propane torch, so you can achieve a thin, crisp top crust without overheating the dessert. You can use the oven broiler instead, but it does tend to overheat the custard. For a variation, substitute other liqueurs, such as Grand Marnier or amaretto.

    4 cups heavy whipping cream
    1/2 vanilla bean
    8 egg yolks
    1/2 cup sugar plus several spoonfuls
    2 tablespoons instant espresso or coffee
    1/4 cup dark rum

Preheat the oven to 325°. Put the cream and vanilla bean in a medium saucepan over low heat and bring just to a boil. Meanwhile, put the yolks, sugar, espresso, and rum in a large bowl and whisk together well. When the cream is hot, remove and discard the vanilla bean, then add a little of it to the eggs while stirring. Add the remaining cream and mix well. Using a large spoon, carefully remove the foam from the surface. When most of the foam is removed, divide the cream mixture among six 8-ounce ramekins or custard cups. Place the ramekins in a roasting pan and fill the pan with enough hot water to reach about halfway up the sides of the ramekins. Put the pan in the oven and bake for about 1 hour, or until a knife inserted in the center of one of the custards comes out clean. Remove the brûlées from the oven and allow them to cool completely, 2 to 3 hours. When ready to serve, sprinkle some of the sugar over the brûlées and place them under a very hot broiler to caramelize the tops. Alternatively, use a propane torch, just until the tops are golden brown, about 1 minute. Serve warm.

Raspberry, Chocolate & Almond Upside-Down Cake

SERVES 12

I hope you find time to sit down with a cup of good coffee and enjoy a slice of this cake right out of the oven. You can substitute strawberries, blackberries, blueberries, huckleberries, nectarines, or peaches, if you like—raspberries just happen to be my favorite. In fact, sometimes I just have a big bowl of them drizzled with warm chocolate sauce and a spoonful of freshly whipped cream. However you prefer your berries, just do as I do—eat lots of 'em!

1 cup firmly packed brown sugar
1/4 cup raspberry liqueur
3 cups fresh raspberries

1 pound bittersweet chocolate, chopped
1/2 cup unsalted butter
1/4 cup granulated sugar

1 1/2 cups ground toasted almonds
   (page 191)
1 cup all-purpose flour
5 eggs, separated
2 cups heavy whipping cream

To prepare the cake, line the bottom and sides of a 10-inch springform pan with aluminum foil. Put the brown sugar and liqueur in a medium sauté pan and cook until melted. Whisk to make a smooth sauce. Pour the sauce in the bottom of the prepared pan and distribute the raspberries over the bottom of the pan. Set aside.

Preheat the oven to 350°. Melt the chocolate and unsalted butter in the top of a metal bowl set over gently simmering water. Remove the pan from the

BERRIES

At the restaurant, we always use fresh berries—strawberries, blackberries, blueberries, loganberries, Marionberries, and huckleberries—in everything from savory dishes to salsas, relishes, and compotes.

The best berries in the world (and lots of 'em) are grown in Oregon. Early in the season, we use California berries because we just can't wait any longer! But once our berries are in season, we usually use them in as many dishes as we can because the season is so short. If I

heat and stir in the sugar, almonds, and flour. Mix well. Add the egg yolks and mix well.

Put the egg whites in the bowl of a heavy-duty mixer and whip until soft peaks form. Gently fold the egg whites into the chocolate batter, using broad strokes.

Put 1 cup of the cream in the mixer bowl and whip on high speed until soft peaks form. Gently fold the whipped cream into the chocolate batter. Pour the batter over the raspberries in the pan.

Place the pan in the oven and bake for 35 to 45 minutes, or until a knife inserted in the center comes out clean. Remove the cake from the oven and let cool for 30 minutes. Invert the cake onto a serving platter.

Whip the remaining cup of whipped cream to soft peaks. Slice the cake, top each piece with a dollop of the whipped cream, and serve warm.

had the space in my freezer I would quick-freeze berries and use them all winter. You can quick-freeze berries for later use by putting the berries on a baking sheet in a single layer and placing it in the freezer. When the berries are frozen, transfer them to reseal-able freezer bags and return to the freezer.

Dark Chocolate Cheesecake with Warm Cherry Compote

SERVES 12

This rich, crustless cheesecake served with cherry compote brings to mind the flavors of Black Forest cake, with that magical pairing of chocolate and cherries. I always use the highest-quality bittersweet chocolate for this, and I recommend using fresh cherries when they are in season. Fresh cherries can be pitted and individually quick-frozen on a baking sheet and then put in freezer bags for use throughout the year.

8 ounces bittersweet chocolate

2 pounds cream cheese, cut into cubes

1 1/2 cups sugar

3 whole eggs

2 eggs, separated

1/4 cup crème de cacao

1 teaspoon pure vanilla extract

CHERRY COMPOTE

2 tablespoons unsalted butter

5 cups fresh cherries, pitted

3/4 cup sugar

1/2 cup brandy

1/2 teaspoon pure vanilla extract

1 teaspoon ground cinnamon

1 cup heavy whipping cream

Mint sprigs

To prepare the cheesecake, preheat the oven to 350°. Butter the bottom of a 10-inch springform pan. In a metal bowl set over a pan of gently simmering water, melt the chocolate.

Put the cream cheese in the bowl of a food processor and process to soften. Stop the machine and scrape down the sides of the bowl. Add the sugar and process again until the cream cheese is very smooth. With the machine running, add the melted chocolate through the feeder tube. Again, scrape down the sides of the bowl and add the whole eggs and 2 yolks. Process to mix. Add the crème de cacao and vanilla and process to mix. Pour the batter into a bowl. Whip the egg whites until soft peaks form. Fold the egg whites into the batter in the bowl. Transfer the batter to the prepared pan and bake in the oven for 1 hour, or until the cake appears set when you gently jiggle the pan. Remove the cake from the oven, let it cool for 10 minutes, then put it in the refrigerator to chill for 2 hours.

To prepare the compote, heat the butter in a medium sauté pan over high heat. When the butter is bubbling, add the cherries, toss with the butter, and sauté for 2 minutes minutes. Add the sugar and sauté for 2 to 3 minutes. Remove the pan from the heat and add the brandy. Return the pan to the heat and add the vanilla and cinnamon. Cook the cherries over high heat until they are tender, about 5 minutes.

Whip the heavy cream to soft peaks. Cut the cheesecake into slices. Spoon some of the cherry compote over each piece, garnish with several mint leaves, then serve.

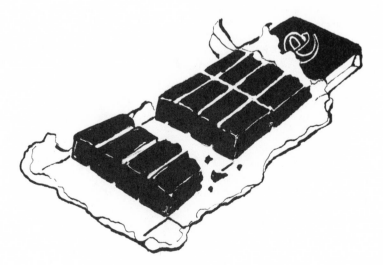

Irish Cream–Chocolate Mousse Cake with Coconut Crust

This dessert is a big hit at the Bistro. It is a dense, serious mousse with a silky texture and an intense chocolate flavor—it has a pound of chocolate in it. I use O'Mara's Irish Cream, which is wine-based and is not as cloying in flavor as the liquor-based Irish creams. This is a big dessert. It fills a 10-inch springform pan to the top.

CRUST

1 1/2 cups Famous Wafer chocolate cookie crumbs

1/2 cup ground toasted cashews (page 191)

1/2 cup ground toasted coconut

1/3 cup sugar

1 teaspoon ground cinnamon

5 tablespoons unsalted butter, melted

FILLING

1 pound bittersweet chocolate

1/4 cup unsalted butter, diced

2 teaspoons instant espresso

4 eggs, separated

1/2 cup sugar

1/2 cup Irish cream

1/2 teaspoon pure vanilla extract

2 cups heavy whipping cream

Mint sprigs

To prepare the crust, butter a 10-inch springform pan. Put the cookie crumbs, cashews, coconut, sugar, and cinnamon in a medium bowl and mix well. Add the melted butter and mix well. Press the mixture into the prepared pan and place in the refrigerator to chill while you prepare the filling.

To prepare the filling, put the chocolate, butter, and espresso in a metal bowl and place over gently simmering water until the chocolate is melted, about 5 minutes. Remove the top of the double boiler and set aside. Do not remove the simmering water from the heat.

Put the egg yolks, sugar, Irish cream, and vanilla in a medium metal bowl (just large enough to nest in the bottom of the double boiler without touching the water) and whisk together. Place the bowl over the simmering water and whisk until the mixture is very thick and resembles softly whipped cream. Fold the melted chocolate and 1 cup of whipped cream into the egg mixture and set aside.

Remove the crust from the refrigerator. In a medium bowl, whisk the egg whites until they form soft peaks but are not dry. Gently fold the whites into the chocolate mixture and pour the mixture into the crust. Refrigerate until completely cold, 3 to 4 hours.

Whip the remaining cup of cream to soft peaks. To serve, cut the cake into slices. Top each slice with a dollop of whipped cream and several mint leaves.

Flourless Orange-Almond Cake with Mocha Sauce

SERVES 10

This moist cake uses 3 cups of ground nuts, which give it body and a soft, chewy texture. The almond extract gives it aroma and a delicate flavor. Use a very good almond extract—and don't use too much, or the flavor won't be delicate at all! I like to serve this cake with fresh fruit.

3 cups blanched almonds, lightly toasted (page 191)

1 cup sugar

1 tablespoon orange juice concentrate

2 teaspoons chopped orange zest

2 teaspoons almond extract

1/2 teaspoon ground ginger

5 eggs

MOCHA SAUCE

1 cup strong brewed coffee

2 cups heavy whipping cream

6 ounces bittersweet chocolate, coarsely chopped

1/2 teaspoon pure vanilla extract

2 tablespoons Kahlúa

COFFEE

The most flavorful coffee is made with roasted whole beans that are ground just before brewing. Freshly ground coffee from a specialty coffee store or a supermarket is also good. The quality of the water you use is just as important as the quality of the beans because each cup of coffee is 90 percent water. Coffee and chocolate go together like peaches and cream. A splash of freshly brewed strong coffee (or a teaspoon or two of instant espresso) can give your favorite chocolate dessert a whole new personality.

Preheat the oven to 350°. Butter a 9-inch cake pan. Place the almonds on a baking sheet and toast them in the oven for about 10 minutes, or until light brown. Remove nuts from the oven and set aside to cool completely.

To prepare the cake, put the almonds and sugar in the bowl of a food processor and process until finely ground. Add the orange juice concentrate, zest, almond extract, ginger, and eggs and process again until smooth. Pour the batter into the prepared cake pan and bake in the oven for about 30 minutes, or until a knife inserted in the center comes out clean. Remove from the oven and let cool for about 10 minutes, then remove the cake from the pan.

To prepare the sauce, put the coffee and 1 cup of the cream in a medium saucepan and heat just until almost boiling. Turn off the heat and add the chocolate, stirring until smooth. Stir in the vanilla and Kahlúa and keep warm until ready to use.

Whip the remaining cup of cream to soft peaks. To serve, cut the cake into slices. Spoon some of the sauce over the top of each slice and top with a dollop of whipped cream.

Apple Custard Tart

SERVES 12

After a hearty meal, we like a simple dessert. In the Northwest, apples are abundant in the fall, and we make lots of apple desserts. This is one of my favorites. The crisp, tart apples contrast with the soft, not overly sweet vanilla custard. It's a pretty dessert, too, with custard poured over the thinly sliced apples; when the tart is baked, the shape of the apples show through. You can serve the tart warm or cold.

TART DOUGH

1 1/3 cups all-purpose flour

1/4 cup shortening

1/4 cup unsalted butter

1/2 teaspoon salt

6 tablespoons cold water

FILLING

4 Granny Smith apples, peeled, cored, and very thinly sliced

1/4 cup firmly packed brown sugar

1 teaspoon ground cinnamon

1 teaspoon allspice

1/2 teaspoon ground nutmeg

2 cups heavy whipping cream

4 ounces cream cheese

1 cup granulated sugar

3 eggs

1 egg yolk

1 teaspoon pure vanilla extract

To prepare the crust, preheat the oven to 350°. Butter 10-inch flan or tart pan with a removable bottom and set aside. Put the flour, shortening, butter, and salt in a medium bowl. Using your fingertips, mix the shortening and butter with the flour to form a coarse meal. Add the cold water and mix the dough with a large fork just until it holds together. You may need to add more water if the dough is dry and crumbly. Wrap the dough in plastic wrap and let it sit for 15 to 30 minutes.

Put the dough on a well-floured work surface and roll out to a 12-inch circle. Place the dough in the prepared pan and bake in the oven for about 10 minutes. Remove from the oven and allow to cool.

To prepare the filling, put the sliced apples in a large bowl. Add the brown sugar, cinnamon, allspice, and nutmeg and toss well. Heat a large sauté pan over medium-high heat. Place the apples in the pan and sauté for 2 to 3 minutes, then remove from the heat and let cool.

Place the spiced apples in the crust in concentric circles, covering the bottom of the crust completely. Put 1 cup of the cream, the cream cheese, and sugar in the bowl of a heavy-duty mixer or food processor and blend or pulse until smooth. Add the eggs, egg yolk, and vanilla, mix well, and pour over the apples. Bake in the oven for about 40 minutes, or until the apples are just tender and the custard is set. Remove from the oven and let cool for 10 to 15 minutes.

Whip the remaining cup of cream to soft peaks. Cut the tart into slices, top with a dollop of whipped cream, and serve.

Lemon Spice Cake
with Caramel-Peach Sauce

SERVES 12

As children, many of us had nearly tasteless raisin-studded spice cake made from a mix. Mark Dowers, our chef at the Bistro, had a different experience. A cafeteria cook at Mark's grade school in Hood River, Oregon, made a fantastic warm spice cake that was so good she inspired him to become a chef. Mark cried when he had to leave that school. Such is the power of good spice cake! Our spice cake is unforgettable, too—it's hearty and has a hit of lemon that brightens the flavors and makes the spices more pronounced. Serve the cake warm with the Caramel-Peach Sauce and a scoop of vanilla ice cream on top. Or, for a completely different result, substitute Blueberry Sauce (page 192) for the Caramel-Peach Sauce.

CAKE

3 cups all-purpose flour

2 cups sugar

1 cup vegetable oil

3 eggs

1/2 teaspoon baking soda

1/2 teaspoon baking powder

1 teaspoon pure vanilla extract

Zest and juice of 1 lemon

1 teaspoon ground cinnamon

1 teaspoon allspice

1 teaspoon ground ginger

CARAMEL-PEACH SAUCE

2 cups sugar

1/2 cup water

4 peaches, peeled, pitted, and diced

1/4 cup dark rum

1/4 cup light Karo syrup

2 tablespoons unsalted butter

1 cup heavy whipping cream or 1 quart vanilla ice cream

Ground cinnamon

To prepare the cake, preheat the oven to 350°. Butter a 9-inch springform pan and set aside. Put the flour, sugar, and vegetable oil in the bowl of a heavy-duty mixer and mix on medium speed just until the ingredients are moistened. Add the eggs one at a time, fully incorporating each before adding the next. Add the baking soda, baking powder, and vanilla, mix well, and then add the zest, lemon juice, cinnamon, allspice, and ginger and mix well. Pour the batter into the prepared pan and bake in the oven for about 45 minutes, or until a knife inserted in the center of the cake comes out clean. Remove from the oven and let cool for 10 minutes. Remove from the pan and set aside on a plate.

To prepare the sauce, place the sugar and water in a large sauté pan and cook over high heat until the sugar starts to turn golden. Do not stir. When the sugar is golden, add the peaches and cook until the sugar dissolves again. Add the rum and Karo syrup and cook until smooth, about 2 minutes. Add the butter and cook until melted, about another 2 minutes. Remove the pan from the heat.

If serving the cake with whipped cream, whip the cream to soft peaks. Slice the cake while it is still warm (or rewarm the cake), and place the slices on individual plates. Spoon some of the hot sauce over each slice. Top with a dollop of whipped cream or a scoop of vanilla ice cream, sprinkle with a light dusting of cinnamon, and serve.

Old-Fashioned Blackberry Cobbler

SERVES 8

This cobbler is a tribute to all the afternoons I spent as a child picking berries and hurrying home to make pie while my mother made jam. I like to serve the warm cobbler with vanilla bean–flecked ice cream.

CRUST

1/2 cup unsalted butter

3/4 cup sugar

3 egg yolks

1/2 cup sour cream

1 1/2 cups all-purpose flour

3/4 teaspoon baking powder

1/4 teaspoon baking soda

1 teaspoon pure vanilla extract

1 tablespoon ground ginger

FILLING

5 cups Marionberries or
other blackberries

1 cup sugar

1 teaspoon ground cinnamon

1/2 teaspoon ground ginger

Zest of 1 lemon

2 tablespoons cornstarch

2 tablespoons unsalted butter

1 quart vanilla bean ice cream

Mint sprigs

To prepare the crust, put the butter and sugar in the bowl of a heavy-duty mixer and mix on medium speed until smooth and creamy. Add the yolks one at a time, mixing well after each addition. Add the sour cream and mix well. Add the flour, baking powder, soda, vanilla, and ginger and mix well. Set aside.

To prepare the filling, preheat the oven to 375°. Butter a 2-quart baking dish or eight 8-ounce individual gratin cups. Put the berries, sugar, cinnamon, ginger, lemon, cornstarch, and butter in a large bowl and toss to mix. Pour the filling into the baking dish, or divide among the gratin cups, and top with the crust, gently spreading the dough to cover the filling. Bake in the oven until the topping is golden brown and a knife inserted in the center comes out clean, about 40 minutes. Remove from oven and cool for 10 minutes.

Spoon the warm cobbler into individual serving bowls. Top with a scoop of ice cream, garnish with several mint leaves, and serve.

Mixed Berry Turnovers with Cinnamon-Vanilla Sabayon

SERVES 12

These turnovers are easy to make and look impressive with all their layers of sweet, luscious fruit inside a crispy, buttery pouch. They are great for brunch or dessert. The warm sabayon made with Tuaca smells so good. You can use brandy or rum in place of the Tuaca, but I recommend using Tuaca because of its complex caramel flavor. I discovered Tuaca on our annual pumpkin-hunting trips with our friend Jeffrey. He would make a drink called Hot Apple Pie, using apple cider and Tuaca. We'd sip these drinks topped with fresh whipped cream and nutmeg while sitting on the tailgate of his station wagon. My son Alex was a baby, and he and his friend Sam would sit on top of a pile of pumpkins in a big wheelbarrow. It was a good time. Jeffrey was a good cook who made many elegant, delicious feasts in remote locations. He passed away a couple of years ago, and we miss him and his cooking dearly.

QUICK PUFF PASTRY

4 1/2 cups flour

2 cups unsalted butter, diced

1 teaspoon salt

1 cup plus 2 tablespoons cold water

FILLING

1 cup fresh raspberries

1 cup fresh blueberries

1 cup fresh blackberries

3/4 cup sugar

2 teaspoons cornstarch

1 teaspoon ground cinnamon

1 teaspoon ground ginger

1 teaspoon allspice

Juice of 1 lemon

2 tablespoons unsalted butter

1/2 teaspoon almond extract

1 egg

1 tablespoon water

CINNAMON-VANILLA SABAYON

6 egg yolks

1/2 cup sugar

1/3 cup Tuaca liqueur

1 1/2 teaspoons ground cinnamon

Dash of pure vanilla extract

To make the puff pastry, place the flour, butter, and salt in a large mixing bowl. Using your fingertips, mix the butter with the flour to form a coarse meal. (It's

continued

Mixed Berry Turnovers *continued*

all right if there are still some large pieces of butter.) Add about 1 cup of the cold water, and mix with a large fork just until it holds together.

Turn the dough out onto a floured board. Form it into a rough rectangle. Fold one-third of the dough toward the center. Fold the other third over toward the center. Turn the dough 90 degrees. Sprinkle with flour and roll out into a rectangle that measures about 20 x 6 inches. Fold the dough in thirds again. Rotate 90 degrees, flour, and roll out. Repeat the process two more times.

Cover the dough in plastic wrap and chill for at least 1 hour. (The dough can also be cut into smaller pieces, wrapped, and frozen.)

To prepare the filling, put all of the ingredients into a medium bowl and mix well.

Roll out the puff pastry dough on a large, well-floured work surface into one 40-inch square or two 20-inch squares. Using a sharp knife, cut out eight 4- or 5-inch squares. In a small bowl, make an egg wash by whisking together the egg and water.

To assemble the turnovers, place about $1/3$ cup of filling in the middle of a square of dough. Fold one corner over to meet the other corner, forming a triangle. Brush the inside edge of the dough with the egg wash. Using your fingertips, crimp the edges well to seal. Brush the top of the turnover with egg wash and place $1/4$ inch apart on a baking sheet. Repeat with the remaining dough squares and filling. Place the turnovers in the oven and bake until golden brown, about 20 minutes. Remove from the oven and set aside to cool slightly while you prepare the sauce.

To prepare the sabayon, put the egg yolks, sugar, Tuaca, cinnamon, and vanilla in the top of a double boiler and whisk together. Place over gently simmering water and whisk until the mixture is light, fluffy, and resembles softly whipped cream, about 5 minutes.

Place the warm turnovers on individual plates, top with the warm sabayon, and serve.

Praline Spice Cookies

The praline bits in these cookies make them both crispy and chewy. For a slightly different flavor, add a couple of teaspoons of orange zest.

3/4 cup pecans, toasted (page 191)
1/2 cup granulated sugar
1/4 cup water
1 cup unsalted butter
1/2 cup firmly packed brown sugar
2 eggs
2 cups all-purpose flour
1/2 teaspoon baking soda
1 teaspoon pure vanilla extract
2 teaspoon ground cinnamon
1 teaspoon allspice
1 teaspoon ground nutmeg
1 teaspoon ground ginger

Spread the toasted pecans on a well-greased baking sheet. Put the granulated sugar and water in a small sauté pan and cook over high heat, without stirring, until golden brown, 3 to 5 minutes. Pour the sugar mixture over the toasted nuts and let cool completely, about 5 minutes. Break the praline into large pieces and place the pieces in the bowl of a food processor. Process until a coarse meal is formed, and set aside.

Preheat the oven to 350°. Butter two baking sheets. Put the butter and brown sugar in a mixing bowl and mix until creamy and fluffy. Add the eggs, one at a time, fully incorporating each one before adding the next. Add the flour, baking soda, vanilla, cinnamon, allspice, nutmeg, ginger, and praline "meal" and mix well. Using a tablespoon, place heaping spoonfuls of cookie dough 1 inch apart on the prepared baking sheets. Bake in the oven until golden brown, about 10 minutes. Remove and let cool before serving.

Caramel Apple–Nut Tart

SERVES 12

This dessert always reminds me of a favorite childhood treat: caramel apples. It's dressed up, but still has the same great flavors. When I was in grade school, each fall my dad would take me to get my allergy shot. Afterwards, we would stop by Morrow's Nut House for a fresh-dipped caramel apple. Years later, when I moved back to Portland and discovered the place was no longer there, I had a good cry. John created this recipe. The tart is a medley of flavor and textural contrasts—tart, crisp apples; spicy-sweet caramel; and crunchy, toasted nuts. We have it on the menu in fall and winter, when local apples are in season.

CRUST
1 1/3 cups all-purpose flour
1/4 cup shortening
1/4 cup unsalted butter
1/2 teaspoon salt
6 tablespoons cold water

FILLING
1 1/2 cups sugar
1/2 cup water
1/2 cup heavy whipping cream
1/4 cup dark rum
1 egg
1 teaspoon pure vanilla extract
1 cup pecans, toasted (page 191)
1 cup macadamia nuts, toasted (page 191)
1 cup hazelnuts, toasted (page 192)
2 Granny Smith apples, peeled and diced
1 teaspoon ground cinnamon
1 teaspoon allspice
1/2 teaspoon ground nutmeg

1 cup heavy whipping cream, or 1 quart vanilla ice cream

VANILLA

Vanilla beans are the fruit of orchids. Of the twenty thousand varieties of orchids, the vanilla orchid is the only one with edible fruit. The three most common types of vanilla beans are Bourbon-Madagascar, Mexican, and Tahitian. About 75 percent of the world's vanilla beans come from Madagascar.

Vanilla extract is the most common form of vanilla. Extracts can be stored for up to one year in a cool, dark place. To make homemade vanilla extract, place a split bean in a jar containing 3/4 cup vodka, seal it, and let it stand for six months.

Fragrant vanilla sugar can be made by burying

To prepare the crust, preheat the oven to 350°. Put the flour, shortening, butter, and salt in a medium bowl. Using your fingertips, mix the shortening and butter with the flour to form a coarse meal. Using a dinner fork, stir in the water, just until the dough starts to come together. Add more water if needed; a wet dough is better than a dough that is too dry. Cover the dough in plastic wrap and let stand for 15 to 30 minutes. Uncover the dough and roll it out into a 12-inch circle on a well-floured work surface. Place the dough in a 10-inch flan pan and bake in the oven for about 10 minutes, or just until set. Remove from the oven and allow to cool. Do not turn off oven.

To prepare the filling, place the sugar and water in a large sauté pan and cook over high heat until the sugar browns, about 5 minutes. Do not stir until the sugar starts to brown. Slowly add the cream and cook until the mixture thickens, about 5 minutes. Add the rum and bring the mixture to a boil. Remove the pan from the heat and set aside to cool completely. When the mixture is cool, stir in the egg and vanilla. Set aside.

Put the nuts, diced apples, cinnamon, allspice, and nutmeg in a medium bowl and toss well. Place the mixture in the bottom of the crust, pour the filling over the top, and shake the pan gently to evenly distribute the filling. Bake in the oven until the center of the tart is bubbling, about 30 minutes. Remove from the oven and let cool about 20 minutes.

If serving the tart with whipped cream, whip the cream to soft peaks. Slice the tart, top each slice with a dollop of whipped cream or a scoop of ice cream, and serve.

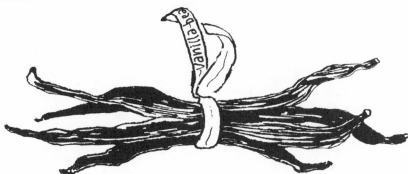

a vanilla bean in a pound of granulated or confectioners' sugar in an airtight container. In two weeks, the sugar will have absorbed the vanilla flavor, which continues to intensify the longer the bean is in the sugar. The vanilla beans keep well and can be re-used. Even when recipes call for simmering a vanilla bean in a syrup or glaze, the bean can be washed, dried, and reused.

When shopping for vanilla beans, choose moist, flexible, firm, and plump ones. The beans are light-sensitive; wrap them tightly in plastic wrap and store in an airtight jar in the refrigerator for 4 to 6 months.

Raspberry Meringue Mountains

SERVES 8

This festive dessert is surprisingly easy to make. The shortbread crust is lined with lime curd, topped with a mountain of raspberries, and covered with a crisp meringue. Your friends will be impressed. You can make a single, larger tart, but the raspberries will fall when you cut it.

CRUST

1/2 cup confectioners' sugar

1/2 teaspoon salt

1 1/2 cups all-purpose flour

1/2 cup ground toasted almonds (page 191)

1 teaspoon almond extract

1 cup unsalted butter

LIME CURD

1 cup freshly squeezed lime juice

Zest of 2 limes

1 1/4 cups sugar

5 egg yolks

2 tablespoons unsalted butter

3 cups fresh raspberries

MERINGUE

5 egg whites

Pinch of cream of tartar

1 cup sugar

To prepare the crust, preheat the oven to 350°. Butter 8 tartlet pans and set aside. Put the confectioners' sugar, salt, flour, almonds, and almond extract in the bowl of a food processor and process to mix. With the machine running, add the butter in the feeder tube about 2 tablespoons at a time. Process until the dough collects on top of the blade. If the dough is too soft and sticky to handle, cover it in plastic wrap and refrigerate until it is firmer and less tacky. Press the dough into the prepared tartlet pans and bake in the oven until golden brown, about 20 minutes. Remove from the oven and let cool.

To prepare the curd, put the lime juice, zest, sugar, and egg yolks in a metal bowl, and whisk together. Add the butter and place over the gently simmering water. Whisk until the curd thickens and coats the back of a spoon. Pour into prepared tartlet shells. Pile the fresh raspberries in a pyramid on top of each tartlet.

To prepare the meringue, put the egg whites and cream of tartar in the bowl of a heavy-duty mixer and mix on high speed until the egg whites are very fluffy. With the machine running, add the sugar about 1 tablespoon at a time until all of the sugar is incorporated. Continue to whip on high speed until the whites are shiny and stiff peaks form. Place the meringue in a pastry bag fitted with a star tip and pipe strips of meringue over the raspberries. To brown the outside of the tartlets, place the tartlets on a broiler pan and brown under the broiler for 2 to 3 minutes. Alternatively, brown with a propane torch held 6 inches away from the tartlets.

Set tartlets on individual plates and serve immediately.

Gingerbread with Caramelized Apples & Lemon Sauce

SERVES 10

CINNAMON

Cinnamon's heady fragrance evokes the best of childhood memories: cinnamon toast. Cinnamon speaks of warm kitchens, comfort food, Christmas, spiced cider, and good cheer. Kids love cinnamon, and sharing it with them is a great way to begin developing their palates. Our appreciation for cinnamon goes back to ancient times, when it came over the trade routes from Ceylon and was highly valued for its ability to mask odors. Romans prized it for its fragrance and dark reddish brown color and used it in aphrodisiac potions. Ancient Egyptians used it for embalming and

In fall and winter, everyone at the Bistro cheers up when I pull the gingerbread out of the oven. The staff shares it warm from the oven with ice cream, whipped cream, and lemon sauce. This good, moist cake, is an updated version of the classic gingerbread I loved as a child. To keep it moist, cut and store it in the pan covered with plastic wrap.

GINGERBREAD

1/2 cup sugar
1/4 cup water
3 Granny Smith apples, peeled and diced
1/2 cup unsalted butter
1/2 cup firmly packed brown sugar
1 cup molasses
3 eggs
3 cups all-purpose flour
1 tablespoon ground ginger
2 teaspoons ground cinnamon
1 teaspoon ground nutmeg
1 tablespoon diced candied ginger
1 teaspoon baking soda
1 cup sour cream
1 cup ground toasted pecans

LEMON SAUCE

3/4 cup freshly squeezed lemon juice
1/2 cup water
1 1/2 cups sugar
Zest of 1 lemon
Dash of pure vanilla extract
1 tablespoon cornstarch
3 tablespoons water
1 tablespoon unsalted butter

1 cup heavy whipping cream

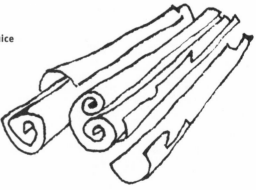

To make the gingerbread, put the sugar and water in a large sauté pan and cook over high heat until the sugar turns golden, 3 to 5 minutes. Do not stir until the sugar starts to brown. Add the apples and cook until they are tender and the caramel is soft, about 4 minutes.

Meanwhile, in the bowl of a heavy-duty mixer, combine the butter, brown sugar, cream, and molasses and mix well on high speed. Add the eggs one at a time, fully incorporating each one before adding the next. Add the cooked apples, mix well, and set aside.

Preheat the oven to 350°. Butter a 9 x 13-inch baking pan and set aside. In a medium bowl, combine the flour, ground ginger, cinnamon, nutmeg, candied ginger, and baking soda. Add half of the flour mixture to the egg mixture. Add half of the sour cream and mix well. Add the remaining flour mixture and mix well. Stir in the remaining sour cream and then add the pecans and mix well. Pour into the prepared pan and bake in the oven until a knife inserted in the center comes out clean, about 45 to 55 minutes.

Meanwhile, prepare the sauce. Put the lemon juice, water, sugar, zest and vanilla in a medium saucepan and bring to a boil. Put the cornstarch in a small bowl and add the water to soften. Whisk the cornstarch into the boiling sugar mixture and then whisk in the butter. Keep the sauce warm until ready to use.

Remove the cake from the oven and let cool for 10 minutes. Meanwhile, whip the cream to soft peaks. Slice the cake and place the slices on individual plates. Drizzle some of the sauce over each slice, top with a dollop of whipped cream, and serve.

herbalists used it to aid digestion. Our name for it comes from the Greek, who in turn borrowed the word from Hebrew traders.

Cinnamon is the inner bark of a tropical ever-green tree that grows in Ceylon and southern India. The bark is har-vested during the rainy season, when it is most-pliable. When it is dry, it curls into long quills that are cut and sold as cinnamon sticks or ground into powder.

I grind my own cinna-mon from cinnamon sticks and use it as soon as possible after grind-ing. I store it ground in a cool, dark place for no longer than one month. Whole cinnamon can be stored for up to one year.

Apricot Tarte Tatin

SERVES 8

This is a classic French upside-down fruit tart, but it's made with apricots instead of the traditional apples or pears. I have also seen it made with peaches. I prefer to use fresh apricots because they are so beautiful and delicious. I love the buttery caramel and the crisp crust. This is a very impressive-looking dessert, but it's not difficult to make. First you make the crust and then you make the caramel and cook the fruit in it. The caramelized fruit goes into an ovenproof tart pan, the crust goes over the top, and the tart goes into the oven to bake. When the tart comes out of the oven, you put a serving plate on top of the pan and turn it over. Voila! You have a beautiful dessert.

CRUST

1 1/4 cups all-purpose flour
1/2 teaspoon salt
3 tablespoons unsalted butter
2 tablespoons shortening
4 to 6 tablespoons cold water

1 cup sugar
1/3 cup unsalted butter
Dash of pure vanilla extract
12 fresh apricots, halved, pitted, and peeled

1 cup heavy whipping cream, or 1 quart vanilla ice cream

To prepare the crust, put the flour, salt, butter and shortening in a medium bowl. Using your fingertips, mix the shortening and butter with the flour to form a coarse meal. Add the water and mix with a fork just until the dough comes together. Cover the dough in plastic wrap and set aside for at least 15 minutes.

Meanwhile, preheat the oven to 425°. Put the sugar, butter, and vanilla in a 10-inch ovenproof sauté pan and cook over high heat until the sugar is golden brown, about 5 minutes. Remove the pan from the heat and arrange the apricots cut side down in the pan. Place the pan on the heat again and bring the liquid to a boil.

While the apricot mixture is heating, quickly unwrap the dough and roll it out into a 12-inch circle on a well-floured work surface. Drape the crust over the apricots and flute the edges with your fingertips. Place the pan in the oven and bake until the crust is golden brown, about 25 minutes. Remove from the oven and let cool for about 5 minutes. Place a large serving platter on top of the pan and, using oven mitts, hold the platter and pan together as you turn the two over, inverting the tart onto the serving platter.

Cut the tart into 8 wedges. If serving the tart with whipped cream, whip the cream to soft peaks. Serve warm with a dollop of softly whipped cream or a scoop of vanilla ice cream on top.

Macadamia Nut Tart

SERVES 12

This Hawaiian-influenced dessert is popular at the Bistro. The subtlety and richness of the coconut and macadamia nuts are perfect together, and they taste delicious with the caramel flavors of the filling. You can substitute other nuts, such as almonds or toasted hazelnuts, for the macadamias, or use a combination.

CRUST

1 1/2 cups all-purpose flour
1/4 cup unsalted butter, diced
1/4 cup vegetable shortening
1/2 teaspoon salt
6 tablespoons cold water

FILLING

1 cup grated unsweetened coconut
2 cups macadamia nuts, chopped
1 cup sugar
1/4 cup water
1 1/4 cups heavy whipping cream
1 egg, lightly beaten
1/2 teaspoon pure vanilla extract

To prepare the crust, butter a 12-inch flan pan with a removable bottom and set aside. Put the flour, butter, and shortening in a medium bowl. Using your fingertips, mix the shortening and butter with the flour to form a coarse meal. Stir in the salt, and drizzle about half of the water into the flour mixture. Stir the mixture with a fork. Drizzle in additional water until the dough comes together. Form the dough into a ball, cover it in plastic wrap, and set it aside at room temperature for 15 to 30 minutes. Preheat the oven to 350°. Unwrap the dough and place it on a well-floured work surface. Roll the dough out to a 12-inch circle about ¼ inch thick. Carefully place the dough in the prepared pan and bake in the oven for about 10 minutes, or just until the dough starts to set. Remove the crust from the oven and set aside to cool. (Do not turn off the oven.)

To prepare the filling, put the coconut and macadamia nuts in the bottom of the cooled tart shell. Put the sugar and water in a medium sauté pan and cook over high heat, without stirring, until the sugar starts to brown. When the sugar begins to brown, slowly add the cream, stirring to incorporate. Cook until the cream turns golden, about 5 minutes. Remove the pan from the heat and set aside until the caramel is completely cool. Whisk the egg into the caramel and pour the mixture over the coconut and nuts in the crust. Place the tart in the oven and bake for 20 to 25 minutes, or until the caramel is set. Remove from the oven and let cool before slicing.

Slice and serve warm, or refrigerate and serve chilled.

Dessert Crepes with Orange Curd

SERVES 10

The first crepes I ever had were at an outdoor art event when I was a kid. They were served rolled up with butter and confectioners' sugar, French-style. I thought I had died and gone to heaven. Then, on my first job out of culinary school, I made one hundred crepes a day! The crepes were made in a huge pan. We would shape them into large cones and fill them with berries, chocolate sauce, and whipped cream. These warm orange curd crepes are delicious. The curd keeps for up to two months in the refrigerator. The crepes can be served with raspberries on top in summer. In winter, try serving them with poached pears.

CREPES

1 1/2 cups all-purpose flour

1 1/4 cups milk

3 eggs

2 tablespoons melted butter

1 tablespoon minced orange zest

Dash of pure vanilla extract

1/4 cup canola oil

ORANGE CURD

1 cup freshly squeezed orange juice

1 tablespoon orange juice concentrate

Zest of 1 orange

1 cup sugar

5 egg yolks, gently beaten

1/4 cup unsalted butter, diced

Confectioners' sugar

Put the flour, milk, and eggs in a medium bowl and whisk well. Add the butter, zest, and vanilla and mix well. Place the bowl in the refrigerator for 30 minutes.

Remove the batter from the refrigerator. In a nonstick pan, heat about $1/2$ teaspoon of the oil, just enough to very lightly coat the pan, over high heat. When the oil is very hot, add about 2 tablespoons of the batter and swirl it in the pan to form a thin, even pancake. Cook for about 2 minutes, or until golden brown. Turn the crepe with a small metal spatula and cook for about 1 minute. Remove the crepe from the pan and set aside on a plate. Repeat with the remaining batter, making about 20 crepes.

To prepare the orange curd, put the juice, concentrate, zest, and sugar in the top of a double boiler and whisk well. Add the butter and place over gently simmering water. Place the egg yolks in a small mixing bowl and gently whisk. Whisk in $1/2$ cup of the hot mixture to temper the eggs. Whisk the warm mixture into the remaining hot liquid in the double boiler. Stir constantly, until the curd is very thick and coats the back of the spoon. Remove from the heat and transfer to a medium bowl. Put the bowl in the refrigerator to chill the curd for about 30 minutes.

To fill the crepes, place the first one on a clean work surface and spoon 1 to 2 tablespoons of the curd in the middle. Fold the crepe in half, then fold in half again to form a triangle. Place on a plate and repeat with the remaining crepes. Place 2 crepes on each plate and dust the tops with confectioners' sugar. Serve immediately.

Caramelized Banana Cream Pie

SERVES 12

Banana desserts don't sell well at the Bistro, but we always run out of this pie.

CHOCOLATE CRUST

2 1/2 cups Famous Wafer chocolate
   cookie crumbs

1/4 cup granulated sugar

1 teaspoon ground cinnamon

5 tablespoons unsalted butter, melted

FILLING

1/4 cup unsalted butter

3/4 cup firmly packed brown sugar

1 teaspoon ground cinnamon

1 teaspoon ground ginger

1/2 teaspoon allspice

4 bananas, peeled and sliced

PASTRY CREAM

3 cups half-and-half

1 vanilla bean, split in half
   lengthwise

8 egg yolks

1/2 cup granulated sugar

1/4 cup dark rum

3 tablespoons cornstarch

1 cup heavy whipping cream

4 sprigs mint

To prepare the crust, butter a 10-inch springform pan. In a bowl, combine the cookie crumbs, sugar, and cinnamon and mix well. Stir in the butter. Press the mixture into the prepared pan and place it in the refrigerator to chill.

To prepare the filling, put the butter and brown sugar in a large sauté pan over high heat and heat until bubbling, about 2 minutes. Add the cinnamon, ginger, allspice, and bananas and sauté until tender, about 3 minutes. Remove the crust from the refrigerator and spoon the bananas evenly over the bottom of the crust. Set aside.

To prepare the pastry cream, put the half-and-half in a saucepan with the vanilla bean and bring to a boil. Remove and discard the vanilla bean. Put the egg yolks, sugar, dark rum, and cornstarch in a bowl and whisk together. When the half-and-half is hot, whisk about 1 cup of it into the egg mixture to temper it. Add the egg mixture to the remaining half-and-half and place the pan over medium heat, stirring frequently, until thick, 3 to 5 minutes. Pour the mixture over the roasted bananas in the crust and refrigerate for 2 to 3 hours, or until well chilled.

Whip the cream to soft peaks. To serve, remove the outer ring of the pan, cut the pie into slices, and top each slice with whipped cream and several mint leaves.

Fresh Fruit Tart with Lemon-Almond Pastry Cream

SERVES 12

Other flavorings, such as mint and orange, can be substituted for the almond. Or, use chocolate pastry cream.

CRUST	LEMON-ALMOND PASTRY CREAM
2 cups all-purpose flour	3 cups half-and-half
1/2 cup confectioners' sugar	1 teaspoon almond extract
1 teaspoon almond extract	Zest of 1 lemon
Pinch of salt	3/4 cup sugar
1 cup plus 1 tablespoon unsalted butter	8 egg yolks
4 ounces bittersweet chocolate	3 tablespoons cornstarch
	Juice of 1 lemon
	4 to 6 cups fresh raspberries, rinsed and dried

To prepare the crust, preheat the oven to 375°. Butter a 12-inch tart pan with a removable bottom. Put the flour, sugar, almond extract, and salt in the bowl of a food processor or heavy-duty mixer. With the machine running, slowly add 1 cup of the butter and process or mix until a dough forms. Press the dough into the prepared pan. Bake in the oven until the crust is golden brown, 20 to 25 minutes. Let cool completely, about 20 minutes.

Meanwhile, melt the chocolate and remaining tablespoon of butter in the top of a double boiler over gently simmering water. Brush the cooled crust with melted chocolate and place in the refrigerator to set.

To prepare the pastry cream, put the half-and-half, almond extract, lemon zest, and half of the sugar in a medium saucepan and bring just to a boil. Meanwhile, put the eggs, the remaining sugar, and the cornstarch in a medium bowl and mix well. When the half-and-half is hot, whisk some of it into the eggs, and then add the eggs to the saucepan. Stirring continuously with a wooden spoon, cook over low heat until very thick, about 5 minutes, never letting it come to a boil. Remove from the heat. Stir the lemon juice into the pastry cream and pour the mixture into the crust. Set aside to cool completely.

Starting along the perimeter of the tart, arrange the berries in concentric circles (rounded side facing up). Slice and serve, or refrigerate until ready to serve.

Basics

Chicken or Turkey Stock

YIELD: ABOUT 1 QUART

2 pounds chicken or turkey bones, rinsed
2 onions, coarsely chopped
2 carrots, coarsely chopped
2 stalks celery, coarsely chopped
3 cloves garlic, chopped
4 sprigs thyme
2 quarts water
1 bay leaf

In a large stockpot over high heat, bring the bones, onions, carrots, celery, garlic, thyme, and water just to a boil. Add the bay leaf. Reduce the heat and simmer for 4 to 6 hours, or until the stock is richly flavored. Strain through a fine sieve into a bowl and use immediately, or let cool to room temperature before refrigerating.

This stock keeps in the refrigerator for up to one week and can be frozen.

Note: To make strong chicken stock, reduce the stock over high heat until about 2 cups remain and the flavor has intensified.

Vegetable Stock

3 onions, coarsely chopped

4 carrots, coarsely chopped

5 stalks celery, coarsely chopped

4 ounces mushrooms, coarsely chopped

4 cloves garlic, chopped

3 shallots, chopped

6 sprigs thyme

2 quarts water

In a large stockpot over high heat, bring the onions, carrots, celery, mushrooms, garlic, shallots, thyme, and water just to a boil. Reduce the heat and simmer for about 1 hour, or until the stock is full flavored. Strain through a fine sieve into a bowl and use immediately, or let cool to room temperature before refrigerating.

This stock keeps in the refrigerator for up to 1 week and can be frozen.

Note: To make roasted vegetable stock, place all the vegetables, the garlic, and the shallots in a large baking dish and roast in a 425° oven for 20 minutes. Add the roasted vegetables to the stockpot of boiling water and proceed as directed above.

Beef, Veal, or Lamb Stock

YIELD: ABOUT 1 QUART

5 pounds beef, veal, or lamb bones

2 onions, coarsely chopped

1 carrot, coarsely chopped

3 stalks celery, coarsely chopped

3 cloves garlic, chopped

2 tablespoons tomato paste

1 cup dry red wine

2 quarts water

1 bay leaf

Preheat the oven to 450°.

In a roasting pan, place the bones, onions, carrot, celery, and garlic and roast for about 1 hour, or until the bones turn golden brown, Spread the tomato paste over the mixture and roast for 10 more minutes. Transfer the mixture to a large stockpot. Add the wine to the roasting pan and, with a wooden spoon, scrape up all of the brown bits from the bottom of the pan. Pour this liquid into the stockpot. Add the water and bay leaf. Bring to a boil over high heat. Reduce the heat and simmer for 6 to 8 hours, or until the stock is full flavored. Strain through a fine sieve into a bowl and use immediately, or allow to cool before refrigerating.

This stock keeps in the refrigerator for up to 1 week and can be frozen.

Note: To make rich veal, beef, or lamb stock, reduce the stock over high heat until about 2 cups remain and the flavor has intensified.

Fish Stock

1 pound fish bones (use bones from whitefish only)

2 leeks

1 tablespoon unsalted butter

2 large onions, coarsely chopped

2 stalks celery, coarsely chopped

2 cloves garlic, chopped

1/4 cup mushroom stems

1 cup dry white wine

4 sprigs thyme

2 quarts water

Coarsely chop the fish bones and place them in a large bowl or stockpot. Cover with cold water and soak for 1 to 2 hours to remove any remaining traces of blood.

Discard the green portion of the leeks. Trim and rinse the white parts thoroughly, then coarsely chop. In a large stockpot over high heat, heat the butter until bubbling. Add the leeks, onions, celery, garlic, and mushroom stems and sauté until they become aromatic, 3 to 4 minutes. Add the wine and bones, decrease the heat, cover the pot, and sweat the mixture for about 8 minutes. Add the thyme and water and simmer, uncovered, for 25 minutes more. Strain through a fine sieve into a bowl and use immediately, or let cool to room temperature before refrigerating.

This stock keeps in the refrigerator for up to 1 week and can be frozen.

Seafood Stock

2 leeks

1 tablespoon unsalted butter

2 large onions, coarsely chopped

2 stalks celery, coarsely chopped

2 cloves garlic, chopped

1/4 cup mushroom stems

1 cup dry white wine

6 cups shrimp, crab, or lobster shells

4 sprigs thyme

2 quarts water

Discard the green portion of the leeks. Trim and rinse the white parts thoroughly, then coarsely chop. In a large stockpot over high temperature, heat the butter until bubbling. Add the leeks, onions, celery, garlic, and mushroom stems and sauté until they become aromatic, 3 to 4 minutes. Add the wine and shells, decrease the heat, cover the pot, and sweat the mixture for about 8 minutes. Add the thyme and water and simmer, uncovered, for 25 minutes more. Strain through a fine sieve into a bowl and use immediately, or let cool to room temperature before refrigerating.

This stock keeps in the refrigerator for up to 1 week and can be frozen.

Roasted Garlic

1 head garlic

2 tablespoons olive oil

Preheat the oven to 250°. Slice about 1/4 inch off the top of the garlic head and discard. Drizzle the oil over it and wrap in foil. Roast until soft, 40 to 50 minutes. Roasted garlic will keep in the refrigerator for 2 to 3 weeks.

Crème Fraîche

2 cups heavy whipping cream
2 tablespoons sour cream

In a small bowl, combine the cream and sour cream, and mix well. Cover and let sit at room temperature overnight. Refrigerate.

Mediterranean Vegetable Relish

1 eggplant, cut lengthwise into
1/2-inch-thick slices
1 zucchini, cut crosswise into
1/4-inch-thick slices
1 yellow squash, cut crosswise into
1/4-inch-thick slices
1 red onion, quartered
2 red bell peppers, roasted, peeled,
seeded, and diced (page 190)

3 cloves garlic, chopped
1/3 cup pitted kalamata olives,
coarsely chopped
2 oil- or salt-packed anchovy fillets
1/4 cup balsamic vinegar
1/2 cup extra virgin olive oil
1 tablespoon chopped fresh oregano
Salt
Freshly ground black pepper

To prepare the relish, brush the grill racks with oil and heat the grill. When the grill is hot, place the the eggplant, zucchini, yellow squash, and onion on it and cook until crisp-tender, 4 to 6 minutes. (The onions will take slightly longer than the other vegetables.) Remove the vegetables from the grill, let them cool for a few minutes, and then dice them and place them in a large bowl. Add the diced bell peppers, garlic, olives, and anchovies, and toss well. Add the vinegar, olive oil, and oregano and toss well again. Season to taste with salt and pepper and let marinate for at least 30 minutes. Use as directed.

Savory Pie Crust

2 1/3 cups all-purpose flour

1/2 cup shortening

1/2 cup unsalted butter

1 teaspoon salt

3 cloves garlic, minced

8 tablespoons cold water

To prepare the crust, place the flour, shortening, butter, salt, and garlic in a large bowl. Using your fingertips, rub the mixture together until a coarse meal forms. Drizzle in the cold water and stir gently with a fork, just until the dough starts to come together. Add a bit more water if needed; it's better to have dough that is slightly wet than dough that is too dry. Cover dough in plastic wrap and let it rest for 15 to 30 minutes.

Roasted Bell Peppers & Chiles

Preheat the broiler. Place the bell peppers or chiles on a baking sheet or in a shallow ovenproof baking dish and broil, turning the peppers or chiles until the skins are evenly blistered and charred, about 15 minutes. Transfer the bell peppers or chiles to a bowl, cover with plastic wrap, and set aside to cool. When the peppers or chiles are cool enough to handle, peel off the skins, remove the stems, and wipe the seeds away. Do not rinse the peppers or chiles under running water because this washes away much of the roasted flavor. Use as directed or drizzle with olive oil and store in an airtight container in the refrigerator for up to 2 months.

Seeded Tomatoes

To seed tomatoes, cut in half crosswise. Cupping one tomato half in the palm of your hand, gently squeeze until all the seeds spill out.

Peeled Tomatoes

To peel tomatoes, bring a stockpot of water to a boil and prepare an ice-cold water bath. Cut an **X** in the bottom of each tomato. Add the whole tomatoes to the stockpot and blanch briefly, 1 to 2 minutes. Using a slotted spoon, transfer the tomatoes to the water bath. When cool, place the tomatoes on a work surface and carefully peel.

Shelled and Peeled Fava Beans

Split open the fava bean shells and remove the beans. Bring a saucepan of water to a boil and prepare an ice-cold water bath. Drop the beans into the pan and blanch for about 30 seconds. Using a slotted spoon, transfer the beans to the water bath. When the beans are cool, drain them. Using a thumbnail, gently pierce the skin of a bean. Slip or peel the skin off and repeat until all beans are peeled. Use as directed.

Toasted Nuts

To toast nuts, place them on a baking sheet and toast in a 350° oven for about 10 minutes, or until they are golden brown and aromatic. Let cool completely, then use as directed.

Skinned Hazelnuts

To skin hazelnuts, toast (see directions above), then wrap in a kitchen towel and set aside to cool. When completely cool, leave the nuts wrapped in the towel and vigorously roll them between your palms until most of the skins have been removed. (It is not necessary to remove all the skins.) Use as directed.

Toasted Spices & Sesame Seeds

To toast spices, place the whole or ground spices in a dry skillet over medium-low heat and toast while stirring continuously. Toast whole spices about 2 minutes, ground spices about 3 to 5 minutes, or until they begin to brown and are aromatic. Remove from the heat and set aside to cool.

Blueberry Sauce

2 cups blueberries
2/3 cup sugar
1 teaspoon freshly squeezed lemon juice
1/2 teaspoon cinnamon

In a small saucepan over high heat, combine all ingredients. Cook, periodically stirring, for about 10 minutes. Transfer to a blender or food processor and pureé. Strain and serve warm or cold.

Sectioned Oranges & Other Citrus

Peel the citrus, removing any remaining white pith. Using a short-bladed knife, cut between the citrus flesh and each side of the membranes separating the sections, letting the fruit slip out of the membranes and into a bowl.

Index